Ha-Meir
La-Aretz Ve-la-Darim

An Anthology of High Holy Day Sermons
Written and Delivered by
Max "Meir ben Isak" Frankel

The title of this book, *"Ha-Meir La-Aretz Ve-la-Darim,"* was purposefully chosen for its double meaning. As Rosh Hashanah and Yom Kippur are the Holy Days most readily associated with the creation of the world and mankind, it is only fitting to acknowledge the Creator in this book's title. In this case, the name for God that was chosen is culled from the paragraph that follows immediately after Borkhu in the weekday and Shabbos morning prayers. In both, God is referred to as, *"Ha-Meir – He Who illuminates."* On a second, deeper and more personal level, the title was also chosen as a way of honoring the author of the sixteen High Holy Day sermons in this book, Max **"Meir** ben Isak" Frankel, who was held in similar esteem by those who knew, respected, and loved him. He continues to illuminate our lives.

May his memory be for a blessing.

זכות אבות לעולם קיימת
The merits of our forebears shall endure forever

Max Frankel **מאיר בן יצחק**, Father

Efraim "Bibi" Frankel, Uncle
אפרים חיים בן יצחק

Hesh Frankel, Uncle
צבי הלל בן יצחק

Walter Neuman, Uncle
שמעון גדליה בן שלום הכהן

Molly Neuman (Frankel), Aunt
מלכה בת יצחק

Leo Frankel, Uncle
אריה יהודה בן יצחק

Helen Frankel (Leeser), Aunt

Isak Frankel,
Father's Father
יצחק בן אפרים

Breintze Golde Frankel (Fenster),
Father's Mother
ברײנצא גאלדא בת אריה יהודה

Efraim Korn,
Father's Zeydie
אפרים

Gittel Miriam Frankel,
Father's Bubbie
גיטל מרים בת צבי אליעזר

Aryeh Yehuda Zeidel,
Father's Zeydie
אריה יהודה

Malka Fenster,
Father's Bubbie
מלכה

Dora Schwab (Frankel),
Father's Tante
דבורה אײדל בת אפרים

Benjamin "Oni" Schwab,
Father's Uncle
ברוך בן עזריאל יצחק

Helen Gottesman (Frankel),
Father's Tante
העטשא בת אפרים

Eisig Gottesman,
Father's Uncle
יצחק אײזיק בן מנחם מנדיל הלוי

Edith Gottesman (Slomowitz),
Father's Cousin's Wife
יהודית בת צבי הירש

Fred Gottesman,
Father's Cousin
אפרים בן יצחק אײזיק הלוי

Lena Frankel,
Father's Tante
דינה לאה בת אפרים

This portrait was taken before Efraim "Bibi" Frankel was the first of his family to escape Nazi occupied Vienna. Bibi sailed to the U.S. on the SS Franconia from Cherbourg on December 24, 1938. Max and his parents left on the SS Saturnia from Trieste on March 2, 1940. They were the last of the family left in Vienna. (L to R: Isak, Bibi, Max, Molly, Hesh, Leo, Breintze Golde)

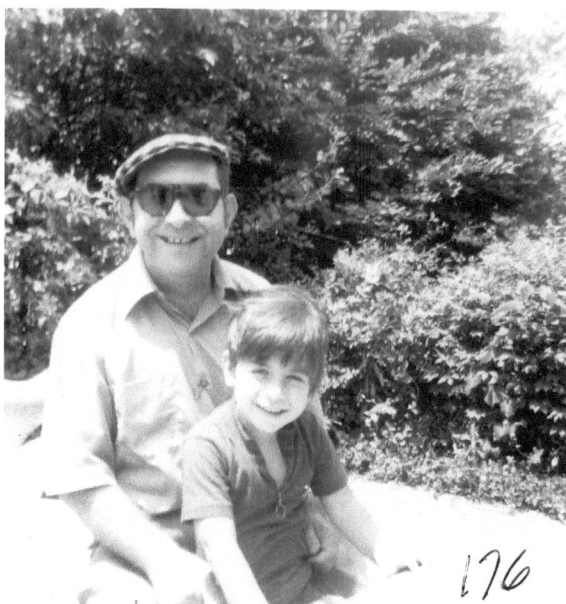

David Frankel, 8, and his father, 47.

Contents

David (l), Danny (r), and Gloria Frankel (not pictured) plant a tree at Camp Livingston in memory of Max Frankel.

Foreword

As I write this brief foreword, I am particularly mindful of two recent trips that my brother Danny and I made to Cincinnati to visit with my mother. The first trip occurred exactly one year ago, and not coincidentally incorporated August 17, 2011, the day that would have been our parents' 59th wedding anniversary. Given that this would have been the first wedding anniversary since my father's passing, we didn't want my mother to be alone. The truth is that we may have needed the trip more than she. In a way that I'm sure is understandable to most, but assuredly to those who've lost a parent, being with my mother on this important day made us feel closer to both of them.

To mark the occasion and bring even greater meaning to our time together, my brother and I prearranged that the three of us would incorporate into our visit the planting of a tree at the same Jewish campgrounds that my father, brother, and I would visit every *erev* Sukkot to cut down scrub evergreens to use as *skhakh* for our homemade wooden *sukkah*. Of course, the tree we planted couldn't be just any tree. Even an evergreen wouldn't do. After making several unsuccessful calls to tree farms in and around Cincinnati, I finally found a nursery that had our intended target, a sweet gum tree. Although it was considerably taller than I preferred, ten feet in all, it was the same kind of tree as the two saplings that my father had planted in front of our home in Cincinnati more than three decades earlier. Over the past several years, the saplings that my father planted have easily grown to 30-40 feet each. Our hope was that the tree we planted at Camp Livingston would meet with an equally successful fate. Surely this would be a fitting tribute to a man who had so carefully "nurtured our roots and tended our branches." And just to be sure this tree planting was unlike any other, we ratcheted up the symbolism by comingling the soil that surrounded its roots with soil I commissioned a friend to bring me from the Old City of Jerusalem. Three months earlier we used a portion of this same Jerusalem soil on my father's *kever* when we unveiled his *matzeivah* (monument) on the occasion of his first *yahrzeit*.

The second trip occurred only a few days ago and once again found the three of us returning to the camp. Feeling a bit like a pilgrimage, we made the trek to see how our tree was fairing and to place a permanent plaque beside its base that identified it as planted in my father's memory. Sadly, the previous year had been unkind to our tree as it had lost nearly all of its foliage as a victim to the tremendous heat and drought that had swept across most of America. Undiscouraged by the turn of events, I was reminded that the saplings my father had planted had a tough go of it as well. Although you'd never know it, one of the saplings planted by my father had even been broken in half by some of the neighborhood kids. I told my brother and mother that I was confident that our tree would overcome its initial adversity just as my father's saplings had so many years before. Indeed, if the soil from Jerusalem hadn't been enough to do the trick, this time around I brought water from Jerusalem to quench its thirst; water that had just a few weeks earlier coursed beneath the Temple Mount and had been collected by a friend at the base of the City of David in the Pool of Shiloah. Yes, I am convinced that our tree, and we, will be just fine. With God's help, the only thing needed by all of us is time. As my father quotes in one of his Yizkor sermons in this sefer, the sage Honi is recorded as having said, "The world into which I was born contained trees my parents planted for me. I plant now for my children."

May the memory of my father, Max "Meir ben Isak" Frankel, be for a blessing, and may my mother, Gloria "Golda bat Shmuel Haim Halevi Hurwitz" Frankel, enjoy the fullness of her years in health and happiness. May they both enjoy the *nahas* they have tirelessly earned as they watch their life's work take root and flourish in the countless generations that descend from each of their children and grandchildren. Amen.

David Tovya Frankel
Elul 5772 / August 2012

Location of the Tree:
+38° 51' 0.05", -85° 6' 32.88"

Bubbie, Zeydie, and their Grandchildren

L to R: Shira, Bubbie, Miriam, Shayna Laya and Zeydie

L to R: Dustin, Sydney, Kaitlyn and Sarah

L to R: Sara, Joshua and Elisheva

The beautiful wood-paneled and stained glass illuminated
sanctuary of Cincinnati's Golf Manor Synagogue

Preface

THE SEFER YOU HOLD in your hands is a time machine of sorts; a device intended to transport the reader back in time and place him in one of the front most pews of Cincinnati's Golf Manor Synagogue to hear the Rosh Hashanah and Yom Kippur sermons first spoken by my father, Max Frankel, a"h, more than three decades ago. Indeed, for nearly all of the 1970s and most of the early 1980s my father had the privilege to facilitate what was known colloquially as the English High Holy Day services at Cincinnati's most well attended Orthodox synagogue. In truth, the worship portion of the services was ably led by a hazzan completely in Hebrew each year. What distinguished my father's service as "English" had much more to do with the flair he had for interweaving into the service his own special blend of translations, explanations, and English responsive readings. It was my father's unique way to make the services more accessible and engaging for the average congregant.

Although he wasn't an ordained rabbi nor formally trained to serve as one, each year my father was recruited by the rabbi of Golf Manor Synagogue, Rabbi David Indich, a"h, to walk 2½ miles each way from our home in Roselawn to lend his considerable talents as the leader of the "standing room only" alternate service that was held in the synagogue's main sanctuary. Those who ordinarily worshiped in the main sanctuary were displaced each High Holy Day season to a full but less attended "Hebrew only" service facilitated by Rabbi Indich in the social hall.

As I read the sermons in this *sefer*, it's not difficult for me to picture my father standing behind the lectern placed high above the congregation as he facilitated the services. I can picture him wearing his white satin *kippah*, his white woolen *tallis* with silver *atarah* for a collar, and his silk *kittel* that started out white but had yellowed over the course of time. In his hands, I can picture the leatherette notebook he carried each year in which he had carefully recorded the choreography for the day. Page X, "Please rise." Page Y, "Please be seated." "Kindly turn to page Z in the book of English supplemental readings that was handed to you as you entered the sanctuary." I can easily remember the resonance of his deep voice as he called out instructions to the congregation. And I can remember how he modulated his voice depending upon the point he was trying to drive home in his sermons. It was a full sensory experience being in my father's service for the High Holy Days. Aside from his rich and pleasing voice and the flutter of sounds that came in each direction from the congregation, there was also the sweet smell of the synagogue's wood paneling, the significant heft of the *mahzor* in my tiny hands, the bouncy feel of the spring loaded seat, and the mesmerizing visage of the two enormous stained glass windows that stared down upon the congregation with their diffused rays of colored light.

As for the sermons that are recorded in this *sefer*, each is a precious treasure. Indeed, in a way that is truly remarkable, his sermons continue to retain their power despite the considerable number of years that have passed since they were first spoken. Although it could be claimed that the universality of the sermon's themes lend to their timelessness, what makes these sermons especially endearing on a personal level is how much they had in common with the dinner conversations in my childhood home. Tempting though it may be to suggest that our dinner conversations were peppered with the topics my father was considering for his sermons, I tend to think it was actually the other way around. My father spoke to his congregation about the same things about which he spoke to his family. In this way, his sermons surely reflected the things about which he cared the most. He spoke of Jewish pride and the critical role love of Israel and Jewish education plays in the identity formation of a committed Jew. He spoke of the scourge of assimilation and intermarriage. He spoke with sadness and frustration about "absentee parents" ... those who denied their children the benefits of a Jewish upbringing because they preferred to spend *Shabbos* at the country club and their Holy Days at ski resorts. He spoke of the difficulty raising *menschen* when so much of our society is polluted by immoral and amoral adults who excel in their vulgarities and indecencies.

And he spoke of a compassionate God who is desperate to forgive his wayward children if only they would show Him the slightest remorse for their misdeeds

Until recently, this collection of 16 High Holy Day sermons rested peacefully in the bottom right desk drawer in my father's private study. And I suspect they would have remained there in silence and solemnity had I not found them quite by accident. My intention in going through his desk drawers (something I still consider taboo) was to make sure I had found and reviewed all of the paperwork he had left behind as we settled his estate upon his recent passing. Little did I know the treasure trove that would be waiting for me.

And the finding of this unique gift came at precisely the right moment. Not a day goes by when I don't think of my father. And not a day goes by when I don't wish but for the opportunity to hear his voice. The gift of this volume is a poor substitute for the man, but in his words I can hear his voice loud and clear. Until such a time comes when my family and I are reunited with my father in the *Olam Ha-Emet*, this volume will take a cherished place among the pictures, videos, and audiocassettes of him that we continue to lovingly catalogue. As much as they are a gift to ourselves, a chance to experience my father and once again feel his love and warmth, they are also a gift to our children and grandchildren that they may better know their Zeydie.

May we heed the words of his sermons and in so doing bring honor to the memory of a wonderful man, Max "Meir ben Isak" Frankel. Amen.

David Tovya Frankel
Elul 5772 / August 2012

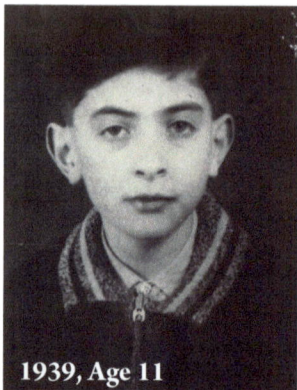

1939, Age 11

L to R: Max and his four sons;
Edwin, Jeffrey, Danny and David

1988

August 17, 1952

2000

August 14, 2000

L to R, Back: Max Frankel, Alvin Warren, Fred Gottesman, Miriam Frankel, Elsa Warren and Hesh Frankel. Seated: Molly Neuman and Leo Frankel

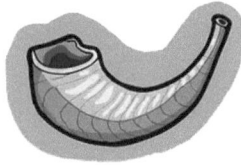

Rosh Hashanah Sermon

OUR TRADITION HAS MANY names for the Holy Day which we observe today. It is Rosh Hashanah, the beginning of the calendar year, but it is also the *Yom Harat Olam,* the day on which the world was conceived and the *Yom Hazikaron,* the Day of Remembrance. It is the day, according to our rabbinical traditions, when Adam, the first man, was created; the day on which Cain and Abel brought their sacrifices to God; the day on which Isaac was bound on the altar; the day on which Jacob had the sublime vision of a ladder reaching to heaven; the day on which God remembered Sarah, Rachel, and the prophetess Hannah and granted them a child; the day on which Joseph was delivered from prison; the day on which the children of Israel were emancipated from Egyptian bondage though their Exodus was delayed until Pesah, the day which witnessed the dedication of Solomon's Temple, and the convocation of the people of Israel who had returned from Babylonian exile to hear Ezra read to them from the Torah scrolls.

It is also *Yom Teruah,* the day of the blowing of the shofar, reminiscent of revelation on Mount Sinai, where amidst the blasts of the shofar and the thunder and lightning, God revealed His law to His chosen people.

But above all, it is *Yom HaDin,* the Day of Judgment, when God, to use the imagery of the prayer book, sits enthroned on the Divine seat of justice, passing all living souls before His almighty tribunal one-by-one, probing their innermost thoughts, meting out justice to all, determining, *"Mi yihyeh u-mi yamut* - Who shall live and who shall die, who shall be at ease and who shall wander, who shall be lowered and who shall be raised."

To our people, now as ever, Rosh Hashanah and Yom Kippur are not merely High Holy Days, but *Yamim Noraim*, Days of Awe, days of trepidation and trembling, days on which the mortal is confronted by the Divine, when God poses to each of us the question first asked of Adam in the Garden of Eden, *"Ayekah - Where art thou?"* and we must answer for our conduct, for our stewardship of the soul which God has bequeathed to us. And there is no hiding from the All-seeing, no answer to the accusation of guilt, "Hast thou eaten of the fruit concerning which I commanded you, you shall not eat of it, for on the day you eat of it you shall surely die."

Who among us does not recall the copious tears which our parents and grandparents shed in the synagogue when the *hazzan* intoned the *u-netaneh tokef, shema koleinu,* and *adam yesodo me-afar.* These were tears of awe and tears of contrition, tears of beseeching and tears of penitence, tears of entreaty and tears of hope. Less sophisticated, perhaps, then we are, less blasé about their religious fundamentals, they viewed the *Yamim Noraim* in concrete, not abstract terms, as the days on which, in fact, their destiny was to be determined for the year to come.

These, then, are solemn days, days not to be taken lightly. The merchant, before the advent of the new season, knowing the public which he serves, examines his shelves and his storerooms, taking inventory of his stock, noting which wares he has in abundance and which are in low supply, what to reorder and what to cancel. So too knowing the God whom he serves, with the approach of Rosh Hashanah the Jew begins to make a *heshbon ha-nefesh,* a spiritual stock-taking, an inventory of his resources of *mitzvot* and *ma'asim tovim* - acts of obedience to God's law and of deeds of loving kindness, on the one hand, and of *aveirot* - sins and transgressions, on the other. But *heshbon ha-nefesh* is not an end in itself. Rather, it is but a preliminary to *teshuvah*, to repentance, to our returning to God with a contrite heart, with sincere regrets for our missteps on life's road, and with earnest determination to mend our ways ere it's too late.

The story is told of Rabbi Yisroel Salanter that he happened, a night or two before Rosh Hashanah, to be walking through the narrow side-streets of his town, when he chanced to notice through the open window of a little hut an old cobbler sitting at his bench and plying his trade by the flickering light of a stub of candle.

Entering, the rabbi remonstrated with the old man. "My friend, you have worked hard all day. You must surely be tired. Put away your shoes. Surely they can wait until morning." "Rabbi," said the old cobbler, "It is true I have worked hard and I am quite tired. But while the candle still flickers, I yet have the opportunity to do a little mending."

Musing, the rabbi left the old cobbler's house and turned his steps toward home. "Lord of the Universe," he exclaimed, "How apt are the old man's words. While the light of life still flickers, while the soul still clings to the body, it is yet time to do a little mending."

Though the mood of Rosh Hashanah is one of solemnity and introspection, the day is characterized not by gloom and despair, but by confidence and joyous anticipation of a favorable verdict from the Divine Judge. Its major theme is life. For Judaism is not a fatalistic religion. The *mahzor* reminds us that, "*Adam yesodo me-afar ve-sofo le-afar* - Man comes from dust and ends in dust." But in his lifetime that spans the beginning and the ending, man is master of his destiny. His fate is determined by the exercise of his free will, not by the workings of relentless forces outside of his own control. In the spiritual as in the other planes of life, man is what he makes of himself.

"I call heaven and earth to witness against you this day," the Torah tells us in the book of Deuteronomy. "I have put before you life and death, prosperity and adversity. Choose life, if you and your offspring would live, by loving the Lord your God, heeding His commands, and holding fast to Him. For thereby you shall have life and shall long endure." But though man may stray from the path which God assigns him, though he errs and sins, the road to reconciliation with God through *teshuvah* is always available, and never more so than on the *Yamim Noraim*. "Repent one day before your death," taught the great Talmudic sage, Rabbi Eliezer ben Horkenos. "Rabbi," exclaimed his students, "Does man know the day on which he is to die?" "Then repent each day as though it might be your last," replied Rabbi Eliezer.

Efficacious though penitence is in finding our way back to God, the *mahzor* prescribes *tefillah* (prayer) and *tzedakah* (charity) as the two other elements required to avert an evil decree. Man lives in three spheres: in his inner being, in his relationship with his Maker, and in his interaction with his fellow human beings. *Teshuvah* (Repentance) is a reordering of the self. *Tefillah* (Prayer) is the acknowledgement of his dependence upon his God. *Tzedakah* (Charity) is the declaration of his social responsibility towards his fellowman. All three elements must be present in man's reconciliation with his God.

Above all, we place our trust in God's loving mercy. Though our merits are few and our deeds unworthy, we look to God as to a loving father. Truly our sins may be many, but His love and his mercy endure forever. It is said that when the great Rabbi Levi Yitzhak, the beloved Berditchever Rebbe, came to the passage in the *mahzor*, "We are filled with sins and You with mercy," he said, "It is true that we are filled with sin yet, how big is Levi Yitzhak, and how many sins can he possibly amass? But You, who are filled with mercy, You are infinite and there is no limit to Your mercy."

In the spirit of the foregoing, on this day of Rosh Hashanah, let us begin to make our own *heshbon ha-nefesh,* let us each probe our hearts and our souls and take stock of our actions of the past year. Let us turn to God with *teshuvah, tefillah,* and *tzedakah.* Let us lift our voices and call on Him to answer our prayers and to grant us His divine mercy, that these *Yamim Noraim* - Days of Awe, be for a blessing for health and for sustenance, for life and for peace, for a release of our brethren from Soviet and Arab bondage, for a world of brotherhood and amity, *ve-Yisrael yashken la-vetah* - a world in which Israel may dwell in safety. And let us say Amen.

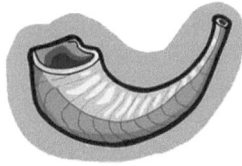

Rosh Hashanah Sermon
A New Year or A New Person

WHEN WE WISH SOMEONE "a happy new year," what word in that greeting are we trying to stress? Is it the word "happy," the word "new," or the word "year"?

It makes a great deal of difference, you know. It may be <u>happiness</u> that we are wishing for ourselves and for others. Or, on the other hand, it may be <u>newness</u> in contrast to sameness that we are hoping for. Or, it may be just <u>another year</u> that we would like to add to the calendar of our lives.

In general, when we deal with time in its relation to life we are dealing with a many-faceted category capable of diverse interpretations.

For many of us, life is an exercise in simple addition. We accumulate years and we spend a lifetime doing it. The Psalmist's appraisal of such a life is well known.

> The days of our years are three score and ten,
> And if by reason of strength,
> They be four score years,
> Yet is their pride but travail and nothingness
> For it is soon gone by and we fly away.

To such as fall within this category, a life span is merely a succession of years. There is no <u>new</u> year for them; just the old year repeated. "Three score and ten" does not add up for such people to seventy years.

For they have not really lived seventy years. They merely lived one year that was repeated seventy times.

At best one might say that many of God's children merely endure but do not live; they grow old but do not age; they cling to the vine of life but never ripen. In the language of our wise men, "people are so afraid to die that they never begin to live."

O, how monstrous are such lives! How drab and colorless they are! How unsatisfying to him who lives such a life and how unproductive to those about him! The same routine, day after day in business, the same preoccupied countenance night after night at home; always too busy for love, for play, for children, for intellectual growth, and for social involvement. God, how many such lives there are! For such there is never a new year, only another year. There is no Rosh Hashanah, only a fiscal period. There is no personality; there are only auditor's figures. The balance sheet of such people may show them to be in the black; their lives, however, are hopelessly in the red.

What a tragedy when man becomes a plodding creature on the treadmill of life! Man was never meant to walk the same weary course day in day out. To register mileage is not enough; one must also cover distance.

At journey's end we need more than respite; we require rest. In our weariness we need more than sleep; we must have dreams.

There is nothing that can drive away the boredom from such a life. Alcohol will not do it. We spent more than thirteen and a half billion dollars on liquor in the United States. A highball does not affect boredom; a cocktail does not break monotony. They may induce temporary gaiety, but not lasting happiness. Sadness, fear, loneliness and depression do not dissolve in alcohol.

Nor can one escape from a bored life and from a monstrous existence. There are some sixty thousand drug addicts in the United States. More than half of them are in New York; fifteen percent in Chicago; and an equal percentage in California. The three most prosperous areas of our country account for eighty percent of drug addiction. It is well to ponder these statistics.

One hundred thousand children are born out of wedlock to teenage mothers in our country. A bored generation, itself looking for thrills, is begetting a new generation that thrives on "kicks" and will get them, no matter what the price.

Well then, is it a <u>new</u> year that we want or some more of the old? What does *"shanah"* mean to us? Repetition? Or something else? Our High Holy Day prayers provide the answer. In those prayers we plead with God "to renew for us a good year." We do not ask for <u>another</u> year but for a <u>new</u> year. It is not repetition that we seek, but renewal. A thinking man is never satisfied with carbon copies of the past. Life for him is not a Xerox machine duplicating page after page of the same script that together becomes an almanac of man's monstrous existence.

If, therefore, we seek renewal, then we must recognize that it cannot be achieved without reflection. Personality renewal, like the renewal of cities, requires planning. Let us see what happened in the case of urban renewal.

All of a sudden many began to realize that the "Blight of Cities" and "Sick Cities" are more than the title of books and articles. They are tragic realities. Slums, crime, delinquency, and other ugly conditions were making American cities almost uninhabitable. Soon came the recognition that there was bad and insufficient housing, not enough parks, unregulated traffic and inadequate facilities for old and young. We then began to grapple with the problem and before long many of the scars will be removed and some of the ugliness will be washed away. Our cities are undergoing a face-lifting job and renewal may prove their savior and the salvation of their residents.

The same is true of personality renewal. That too begins with reflection. Here is how it frequently works. There comes a moment when a man takes a sharp look at himself and doesn't like what he sees. He discovers what greed has done to his character and what unbridled ambition has done to his health. He begins to understand that his rages and hostilities were not really directed at others but were manifestations of dissatisfaction and disappointment with himself.

From reflections upon himself as a man, he turns to thoughts about himself as a Jew. He looks into his home and realizes what he should have known for some time that something precious has departed from it. He recalls his ancestral home and knows that his own is so different. What, he wonders, has happened to the Friday nights at home, to the holy atmosphere that prevailed in it; to father's *kiddush*; to mothers halo as she lit the *Shabbos* candles; to the lusty voices of children chanting the ancient melodies round the family table?

His reflections continue. What has happened to so many sacred and precious institutions – the kosher table, the Passover *seder*, the High Holy Day climate. Nostalgia overcomes him as he remembers the *Kol Nidre* night of his childhood days. He recalls how children clustered round a parent or grandparent, heads lowered to receive the paternal benediction. On mantelpiece or sideboard glistened the lights kindled as memorials to the departed family forebears. The living and the dead seemed to form one continuous and united household.

As he reflects upon these things he begins to understand what they meant, and what their disappearance caused. These rituals and symbols made the Jewish home at once a sanctuary and a fortress of Judaism. They were the ramparts against assimilation and the safeguards against intermarriage. They provided a sacred setting and a holy environment where love was cultivated, fidelity was inspired, and reverence for God, parent, and fellow man were taught.

The thinking man and the serious Jew must realize that from many homes all this is gone. And what is the result? More divorces, more intermarriage, more social climbing and more vulgar status seeking!

We had all better take a good look at ourselves. We will then not be content with just another year and with more of the same. Our prayer will be, *"Haddesh yameinu ke-kedem* – Renew our days as old." We will heed the advice of our sages, *"Ba-hodesh ha-zeh te'hadshu ma'aseikhem … Ba-hodesh ha-zeh shapru ma'aseikhem* - Renew your actions; improve your deeds." We will be done with repetition; we will engage in renovation.

There is, however, something that is superior even to renewal or renovation. Renewal when applied to a city or to a personality may be compared to a patch that is sewn into a garment. The hole does not show; not because it is not there, but because it is covered up. The patch and the original fabric simply do not match. The wearer knows it and before long others discover it too.

Patch the human personality and presently, fresh rips and tears will appear. Even if on the surface all remains well, there is always the possibility that beneath the patch, festering sores will develop and pockets of infection will breed. Psychiatrists call that which is under the patch, the subconscious. They know the havoc that is caused when conditions of that sort are permitted to smolder within the deep caverns of the human mind. Before long poisons pollute the personality and dangerous fumes suffocate and strangulate the soul. Renovation or renewal treats a symptom; it does not grapple with the cause. To overcome the cause of human error, to eradicate evil from the human heart, and to eliminate the inclination to sin, we must strive for the transformation of personality. It simply does not make sense for an intelligent person to behave badly for three hundred and sixty four days, and then atone for them in one day. Prolonged misconduct cannot be dealt with that way. If that is so then our goal must not be simply <u>another</u> year; that is repetition. Nor should we be satisfied with a <u>new</u> year; that will merely be temporary renovation. We must seek and pray for a <u>different</u> year; yes, an altogether different year.

Did you ever watch the members of a track team as they are rehearsed for the break away. "On your marks, get set, go," the coach repeats endlessly. Always there must be a fresh and perfect start if there is to be a good race and a victorious finish. So it is with life. We need a fresh start if we are to become different personalities.

The prophet Ezekiel understood this well. The Babylonia of his day was big, cosmopolitan, pagan and tempting. The Jewish exiles from Palestine who but yesterday wondered about how they can "sing the Lord's song in a foreign land" somehow adapted themselves too well to their new environment. They succumbed to the blandishments of the surrounding culture and many fell prey to the corrosive influences of assimilation to which every minority is exposed. Before long the prophet Ezekiel looked upon the Jewish community of Babylonia as a "valley of dry and dead bones."

To save the remnants of that community the prophet realized that half-measures would not do. An occasional visit to a sprawling synagogue in suburban Babylonia will not restore the wilted and atrophied soul of an alienated Babylonian Jew. Nor will membership in the Jewish country club of Nineveh inspire Jewish pride and cultivate a sense of identity with one's people, with its former homeland and with its promised redemption.

What was needed, the prophet concluded, was a total transformation of the Jewish personality. And transformation is what Ezekiel preached, *"Ve-natati la-khem lev ve-ruah hadashah etein be-kirbakhem* - And I will give you, he said in God's name, a new heart, and a new spirit will I implant within you." Nothing short of that will do. The prophet makes his thought even clearer, *"Va-hasiroti et lev ha-even, mi-besarkhem, ve-natati lakhem, lev basar* – I will remove the heart of stone from out of you, and I will give you a heart of flesh."

Here is the first case on record of a spiritual heart transplant. You dare not leave "the heart of stone" and treat it periodically with spiritual nitroglycerine or with doses of religious digitalis. Nothing short of a "new heart" and a "new spirit" will result in a new personality.

Maimonides in his Laws of Repentance punctuates this thought as only a Talmudic genius who was also a master physician can do. Real penitence, he suggests, means total reconstruction; virtually rebirth. *"U-meshaneh shemo, ke-lomar ani aheir ve-ani oto ha-ish she'asah otam ha-ma'asim … ve-goleh mimkomo* – The penitent should change his name, indicating thereby, 'I am someone else; I am no longer the man who did the former things.' He should even leave his place of residence and go elsewhere."

What an insight! To become a different person one most undergo a complete metamorphosis, a cataclysmic change of character, a psychic revolution. One must assume a fresh identity and move into a new environment. He who would transform his personality as a man and as a Jew must be willing to change his ways, his friends, his outlook – yes, even his address.

This applies as well to society as a whole. As a society we have been makers of war, we have been witnesses to pernicious poverty in our own country and abroad, and we must put an end to that. We have been indifferent onlookers to those evils of racial inequality, and we must no longer tolerate that. We must acknowledge the sickness of our society and determine to heal it, to transform it, and in the process to transform ourselves.

We must do the same as Jews. The kind of Jews that some of us have been we dare no longer be. We must assume a new identity, which means a return to our original identity. Let us ask ourselves the simple question, who are we? Obviously we are Americans and justly proud of it. We live in comfort and security in this blessed land and we thank God for our good fortune. But who really are we? We are the descendants of Rabbi Akiva. The sages, prophets, psalmists, philosophers of Judea and of medieval Europe are our ancestors. Every major faith of mankind sprang or borrowed from our faith. The six million who were exterminated but yesterday were our brothers. The heroes who saved a Jewish state and saved two million of their countrymen from threatened annihilation – these heroes whose daring and imaginative rescue of the hostages of Entebbe revived the lagging spirits of Israel and taught the world a new lesson of morality – they are our kinsmen. See who we are; what our true identity is? Let us glory in that identity. Let us shed the protective resemblance, the camouflage that conceals our true selves. *Hashlihu ma'aleikhem, et kol pisheikhem asher p'shatem bam va-asu lakhem lev hadash, ve-ruah hadashah* – Cast away all your errors and acquire a new heart and a new spirit." It is not <u>another</u> year that we need as Jews, nor even a <u>new</u> year. The Hebrew word *"shanah"* which means <u>year</u> and which means <u>to repeat</u> also means <u>to change</u>. It is a change of transformation that we need, a fresh start towards Jewish living.

The Universal Coach seems to stand over us with the watch of destiny in his hand, calling to us, "My children, get on your marks, get set, go." God speed to us all.

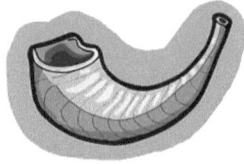

Rosh Hashanah Sermon
1974

THE THEME OF REMEMBRANCE runs like a constant refrain through the Rosh Hashanah liturgy. Our Torah reading this morning, in speaking of the birth of Isaac, opens with the phrase, *"Ve-Hashem pokeid et Sarah -* God remembered Sarah."   Similarly, the Haftarah tells of God's remembering Hannah and the birth of Samuel. The motif of *Zikhronot* (Remembrance), is one of the three major themes of the Amidah. Phrases such as *Zakhreinu le-hayim* (Remember us for life), *Zokheir ha-brit* (He who remembers the covenant), *Zakhreinu be-zikhron tov le-fanekha* (Remember us favorably), abound in the service. Indeed, one of the names by which Rosh Hashanah is known is *Yom Hazikaron* (the Day of Remembrance).

Why this emphasis on remembering? What is the significance of this theme for the High Holy Days?

On Rosh Hashanah the theme of *Zikhronot* bids us to look into ourselves and to call to mind our deeds of the past. For through *heshbon ha-nefesh*, through reflecting on our actions, our moral failings and ethical shortcomings, we may be moved to *teshuvah*, to contrition and repentance, which in turn may win us Divine forgiveness.

But our *Zikhronot* are also an appeal to God, who remembers all forgotten things, to grant us a favorable verdict, if not for our own merits, *"Ki ein banu ma'asim -* for we are deficient in good deeds" then *"be-zekhut avot* - for the merits of our ancestors," the Patriarchs and prophets, the scholars and martyrs, whose memory we invoke.

But, I would submit to you, there is another dimension, and that is an inwardly-directed dimension that speaks to us individually and as a people and bids us to remember. For essentially we are individuals and we remain a people only in so far as we maintain our memories. Remove our memories, and we are naught. Our memories not only shape what we are, but we are because we remember.

There is probably no more tragic figure than an individual suffering from amnesia. The trauma that strips the amnesiac of memories strips him of his identity. Not knowing who he is and whence he came, not knowing his family and his friends, lacking guideposts of past aspirations and experiences, the man without a memory moves in a mental and spiritual vacuum, adrift without direction. No amount of material comfort, no measure of physical effort can alleviate his plight. Only restoration of his lost memories can bring back his identity, and with it his purposeful existence. So it is with nations. We are Americans because of our American memories. Whether we came on the Mayflower or on the last flight from overseas, whether our memories are first-hand or vicarious, we are Americans because of American memories. Our memories may not be detailed, but if they are an essential part of our conscious and our sub-conscious self, then they animate and motivate our existence, and we are Americans. We were there at the Boston Tea Party and drafted the Declaration of Independence with Jefferson. We drove the wagons west and civilized the wilderness. We agonized over the fratricide of the Civil War, and opened our shores to the flood of the downtrodden. We fought to make the world safe for democracy, stormed the beaches at Anzio and at Iwo Jima. These are but a few of our national memories. Each one of you here could easily elaborate on them.

But national memories aren't all there is. There are also our individual memories, of good times and bad, of struggling to establish ourselves, of the hardships of depression and the rough climb back to normalcy, of our first car and of our first home, of trips we have taken and places we have seen. We are the composite, the end product of these memories.

But America is young. We are still two years away from celebrating the first two hundred years of our national existence. What shall we say of our national memories as Jews -- memories stretching back over the span of four thousand years. Our people's memories extend not only in time -- they extend in space -- for there is hardly a country in the world, hardly a spot on the globe in which our people have not played a role. From Abraham to Moses, from Solomon's empire to the Babylonian and Roman dispersions, from the Spanish inquisition to the Chmielnicki massacres, from the handful of Jewish settlers in New Amsterdam to the mightiest Jewish community in the world, from the furnaces of Auschwitz to the heights of the Golan -- our memories are a rich tapestry of inspiration and dedication, of courage and idealism. Our national memories as Jews transcend places and events, and focus on the heroes of our history -- Patriarchs and judges, prophets and priests, scholars and fighters, the thousands upon thousands of men -- and women as well -- of courage and of spirit, who imbued our people with its sense of holiness and purpose, who impressed upon us our mission to be a light unto the nations and whose courage and steadfastness imprinted the Jewish presence on the fabric of the world's history.

And what of our individual, personal memories? To be a Jew encompasses the many experiences and acts in which from childhood we have been participants, and which personalize and give meaning to our individual expression of Judaism. Blessing the candles, chanting the *kiddush,* building a *sukkah,* finding the *afikoman,* that first fast on Yom Kippur, the Jewish National Fund box and the Israel Independence parade, Hebrew School and Jewish cultural activities, dancing *a freilach* at a wedding, these are the building blocks of our individual memories. *Yom Hazikaron* (the Day of Remembrance), reminds us that we are who we are and what we are, that we retain on collective and individual identity as Jews only as we remember. This is why we have, over the ages, so valiantly resisted every oppressor's efforts to close down our schools and to put an end to our religious observances. For our national consciousness realized that should our enemies succeed in depriving even one generation of the knowledge of our past and of the rituals and observances that unite us with our people through time and space, that chain of memories going back to our very beginnings as a people would inevitably be broken, and like the amnesiac we would be reduced to a pitiful condition of aimlessness and identity-less existence in a bewildering world beyond our comprehension.

On this *Yom Hazikaron* of 5735 this is the greatest challenge facing us as a people and as individuals. We must not let apathy and indifference dim the memories that for centuries have given meaning and purpose to our existence. We must strengthen the institutions of learning that are the storehouses of our memories. We must make sure that our children receive a thorough Jewish education, ranging beyond the elementary years into the high school years and into adult life, so that we can transmit to them our national memories. We must, ourselves, reinvigorate and renew our ties with our Jewish past, by picking up a Jewish book, by attending an adult education class, by taking an active interest in the life of the Jewish community at home and abroad. We must provide for ourselves and for our children the daily experiences of Jewish living in the home and in the synagogue.

In today's Torah portion we read, *"Ve-Hashem pokeid et Sarah -* God remembered Sarah." Now the word *pokeid* is not the common word for remember, as those of you who know Hebrew well know. The regular word for remember is *zakhor.* Why *pokeid* in this Biblical verse? Because the word *pokeid* has another connotation. It also means appointed, commanded, invested with a responsibility. In granting Sarah her long longed-for son, God invested Sarah with the responsibility of instilling in him the traditions of her household, the traditions of Abraham, for through him was God's design for the seed of Abraham to be transmitted to generations yet unborn. Her seeming ruthlessness in driving Ishmael and Hagar away, may be understood as a reflection of her concern lest Isaac be exposed to bad influences that would lead him astray from Abraham's teachings.

This responsibility, so deeply felt by Sarah, rests upon the shoulders of all of us whom God has remembered and blessed with the gift of children. Parenthood imposes upon us the obligation to rear our children with positive Jewish memories, the *Zikhronot* of our national heritage of scholarship and culture, of heroism and martyrdom, of faith and righteousness, and the *Zikhronot* of the Jewish home, the memories of the simple daily acts of Jewish living that in their totality are the measure of our Jewish identity and commitment.

We pray that on this day of remembrance we all be remembered for good, for life and health, for peace and blessing. And may the dawning of the new year reawaken in us the memories of our past, as we dedicate ourselves to building for ourselves and for our children, memories for the future, that we may live. Amen.

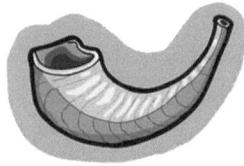

Rosh Hashanah Sermon
1975

To THE PAGAN PEOPLES of the ancient Near East, the new year was a time of fear and despair, a dread period during which vindictive demons and evil spirits were abound. Prudent men shut themselves up in the safety of their homes, hoping to escape the notice of gods and demons alike, or raised a huge din to drive away the lurking spirits.

How very different is our conception of Rosh Hashanah! A day of judgment – yes. A day of solemnity and awe – yes. But not a day of gloom, filled with a sense of impending disaster, not a day of helpless and mute acquiescence in the inevitability of doom. On the contrary, a spirit of optimism permeates the High Holy Day season, a deep conviction that the Almighty Judge will temper justice with mercy, and abiding faith that the decree of the Divine tribunal will be favorable, and that we, through our prayers, our resolves and our actions can affect the outcome of heavenly proceedings.

Not death, but life, is the underlying theme of our High Holy Day prayers. *"Ne'um Adonai Elohim, Im eh potz be-mot ha-rasha, ki im be-shuv rasha mi-darko, ve-hayah* – So says the Lord God, I have no pleasure in the death of the wicked, but that the wicked turn from his way and live." Our prayers characterize God as *Elohim Hayim* (God of life), *Melekh Hafetz Ba-Hayim* (a King Who desires life), and Who will, in His abundant mercy inscribe us in the Book of Life for His Name's sake.

But God's judgment is real enough, and while we express optimism about the outcome, we are also conscious of our frailty, aware of our inadequacy, and concerned with how we measure up to the imperatives of our faith.

Rosh Hashanah reminds us dramatically that the moral and spiritual values of our faith are absolutes and that we are accountable for our conduct as free moral agents. In our age, when it has become fashionable to be cynical, to look at everything – religion and morality emphatically included – as relative and consequently as not binding, the Day of Judgment shocks us into facing the reality of sin and its consequence. Sin is disobedience to God's commandments, acts of omission or commission against the Divine Will as revealed in the Torah and transmitted through countless generations of the Jewish people. Judaism teaches that man is born pure with a free will to choose his moral path. We make our own choices and we must take responsibility for our actions since they are of our own choosing.

And yet, if poor mortals that we are, we choose poorly, if we have strayed from the teachings of our faith, we need not despair. Our doom is not automatic. We have the means to change the evil decree. Rosh Hashanah gives us a second chance: to erase the past, to make our peace with God, to begin anew. How? Our prayer book lists three words that spell out a formula for reconciliation with God; *teshuvah* (repentance), *tefillah* (prayer), and *tzedakah* (righteous living).

What is *teshuvah*? The word *teshuvah* comes from the root meaning "to return." The act of *teshuvah* is not merely a feeling of remorse, of vague regret, of humbled well-meaning resolutions. *Teshuvah* to be meaningful must involve genuine spiritual return to the Source of our being, a full and contrite renunciation of our sins, a genuine commitment to mend our ways. It partakes of the quality of what the prophet calls "making us a new heart" to serve the Lord in truth. *Teshuvah* cannot be a mere formality, a mouthing of pious phrases. Surely He Who searches our hearts on the Day of Judgment is not to be deceived. Yet, when *teshuvah* is genuine, there is no greater force, no greater good in the world.

Our rabbis taught, *"Makom she-ba'ali teshuvah omdim tzadikim gemorim einam omdim* - The place occupied by the true penitent is greater than that occupied by a saint." And again, *"Yafeh sha'ah ahat be-teshuvah mikol hayai ha-olam ha-ba* - An hour of *teshuvah* is to be treasured more than life eternal in the world to come."

The efficacy of *teshuvah* is perhaps best seen in the story of Jonah that we read at the *Minha* service of Yom Kippur. While most of us may remember the story best as the tale of a man who was swallowed by a big fish, the true importance of the story is in Jonah's mission, a mission which he attempted to escape, and which he finally, reluctantly, and against his will carried out. He was sent by God to Nineveh, a heathen city of Assyria that wallowed in sin, to preach to the inhabitants that destruction was imminent as a consequence of their sin and to exhort them to *teshuvah*. Jonah did not want to spare the sinners. He wanted them doomed. But when the inhabitants of Nineveh heeded God's message, and repented, the city was spared. Not even the hardened sinners of heathen Nineveh are beyond God's mercy.

When is the proper time for *teshuvah?* We generally consider the ten-day period between Rosh Hashanah as the *Aseret Yamei Teshuvah,* as the Ten Days of Penitence. Jewish tradition assigns a special significance to these days. They are *Yamei Ratzon,* Days of Divine favor. But truly, the time for *teshuvah* is anytime. The rabbis taught, *"Sha'arei teshuvah tamid niftahim* - The gates of penitence are always open."

You may remember the story of Eliezer ben Hyrcanus who is reported in the Talmud to have advised his students that they should repent an hour before his death. "Rabbi," said the students, "does man know when he is to die?" Rabbi Eliezer's reply is classic: "Regard each hour as though it may be your last." *Teshuvah,* then, true and genuine repentance, is the first condition to reconciliation with God.

Tefillah, prayer – is the second. There are many expressions and words in Hebrew that connote prayer. They range from entreaty to praise to thanksgiving to supplication. And yet the best-known word in Hebrew is *tefillah.* It is a most interesting word. Its assigned meaning is reciting the mandatory services. In this sense it partakes of the general meaning of what we refer to as prayer – the reading of the hymns of praise, the chanting of the Shema, the silent devotion, and all the other portions of the daily service.

But its root meaning is altogether different because the root meaning of *tefillah* is *pallal,* to judge. And it is particularly significant that the verb form of the word is always conjugated in the reflexive – *le-hitpallal* – literally, to judge oneself. All of which helps us to understand a dimension of prayer that is unique to Judaism. Prayer is not only reading prescribed verses, but more importantly, it is a process of searching one's own soul, of *heshbon ha-nefesh* of self-scrutiny, of trying to measure up, to determine our worth, as we stand before the Almighty and ask His forgiveness.

Prayer that is merely mumble, merely cant, is no prayer. Rabbi Simeon advises us in Pirkei Avot – *Ke-sha'atah mitpallel* (When you pray), *al ta'as tefillatkhah keva,* (regard not your prayers as a routine task), *elah rahamim hanunisut lifnei HaMakom* (but as an appeal for mercy and grace before the All-Present).

Tefillah, self-scrutinizing prayer, helping us to know ourselves, our shortcomings, our imperfections better, is not merely a second condition for reconciliation. It is an essential step toward genuine *teshuvah.*

And the final word in the formula is *tzedakah.* Its best-known translation, *tzedakah,* means charity and certainly deeds of kindness towards our fellow man. Charitable instincts are most highly regarded in Judaism, so highly regarded, indeed, that the Book of Proverbs says, *"Tzedakah tatsil me-mavet* - Charity saves from death."

But in its larger sense *tzedakah* is not charity. Charity smacks of a patronizing attitude. The hand-out makes the giver feel smug and self-satisfied. Look at what a great guy I am! Look how charitable, how good to my fellow man I am.

Tzedakah is a form of the word *tzedek,* righteousness. Righteous living is the essence of Judaism. The Torah and the prophets, in countless passages, exhort us to practice righteousness in our relations with our fellow man, in our social life, in our business life, in the administration of justice, in every aspect of our daily existence.

"Tzedek, tzedek tirdof," says the Torah. Pursue righteousness. Don't stand by waiting for it to come to you – go after it vigorously. And the repetition of the word *tzedek* in the opinion of a noted commentator connotes that not only the end results of our undertakings must be righteous, but the means to their attainment must be equally righteous.

Tzedakah then is not the mere giving of alms, but the understanding that in the act of helping my fellow man I am performing an act of righteousness that is his due. That in pursuing the aims of social justice, in righting the wrongs of my fellow man, in conducting my affairs with scrupulous honesty and concern for my fellow man, I am simply obeying a fundamental tenet of my faith. And in passing, we may note that *tzedek* and *tzedakah* is more often than not coupled in the Bible with *mishpat,* justice. Righteousness and justice go hand in hand. Righteousness is the justice due to our fellow man. *Teshuvah, tefillah,* and *tzedakah* is the formula for reconciliation with God, and the means to averting the evil decree.

No matter how far we may stray, a return to these tenets will anchor us once more securely to our faith and to the Author of our destiny.

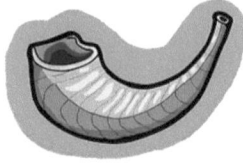

Rosh Hashanah Sermon
1976

IF YOU WERE ASKED to draw a symbol that would identify the Torah scroll as on object of religious reverence, what would you choose? A few years ago, our Tikvah Juniors Sunday school class which consists of children with physical, emotional, and intellectual disabilities was studying a lesson about the Torah. Patiently the teacher tried to discuss with the children what the Torah is. She showed them a beautiful film on how a Torah is written and how it is employed in the services. She took the class to the chapel where the rabbi obligingly removed a scroll from the ark, opened it, chanted a few verses, and let the children inspect it closely. Then it was back to the classroom, where the children were given outlined pictures of on open Torah scroll to color in. To see if they had understood the lesson, the teacher asked them to mark the picture with some symbol that would identify it as a sacred religious object. One of the children hastened to comply and marked it with the symbol that conveyed religious significance to him. He drew a cross. In thinking about a sermon topic for Rosh Hashanah, I was reminded of this incident, and wondered how the child's parents – how all of us – would have fared had we been asked to do what these children were told to do.

For more often than not, in matters trivial and important, at home, in our synagogues and communities, wittingly or unwittingly, we superimpose the views and doctrines and practices of the church on the rock bed of our faith. Without realizing it, we draw a cross on our Torah.

In the process of adapting to our gentile environment as a minority people in an alien culture, we convert our synagogues into Jewish cathedrals, our rabbis into Jewish parish priests, our Sabbaths into weak imitations of the Christian Sunday, our homes into religiously sterile replicas of our gentile neighbor's, and our children into religious blanks who are not too far out of step with the mores of the Christian world. Mostly we do it in all innocence, without awareness. And this is because we have been conditioned to accept as universal truths basic Christian tenets that are diametrically opposed to the traditional Jewish outlook on life. From our Christian neighbors we have borrowed the concept of religion that compartmentalizes life into distinct and separate domains: the one labeled "religious" and the other "secular." The church's main preoccupation is with the so called "religious" aspect of life, defined as man's relationship with God, with the salvation of his soul from eternal perdition, with a view of spirituality and holiness which are a repudiation of the world of the everyday and a retreat from the here and now, and with prayer, sacraments, religious rites, and affirmations of faith. It is the latter, in particular – the affirmation of faith – which is the prime prerequisite of Divine grace which alone can "save" sinful man from eternal damnation. Man's deeds, however meritorious, are beside the point. Nor can man reach salvation completely on his own. The priest or minister is an indispensable intercessor, imbued with esoteric knowledge and with special powers and religious authority that transcends those attained by ordinary mortals. Indeed, Christian theology's understanding of salvation is preoccupied to the point of obsession with the next world in place of the here in now, with the soul at the expense of the body.

How vastly does the Jewish conception of the world and man's place in it differ! Follow the prayers throughout these High Holy Days and these differences become readily apparent. Life is not compartmentalized, but is an organic whole. Judaism does not differentiate between the religious and the secular. Judaism cannot accept the dictum "Render unto Caesar that which is Caesar's and unto God, that which is God's." For all of man's concerns are legitimately the province of the Jewish way of life. If anything, Judaism is more concerned with the material world than with the spiritual; the commandments regarding obligations between man and his fellow man, *"Bein Adam Le-haveiro,"* far exceed those regarding obligations between man and God, *"Bein Adam Le-Makom."* The world of the here and now takes precedence over the world of the hereafter. While hoping for God's salvation and for the rewards of *Olam Haba,* the World to Come, we are enjoined, *"le-takein olam be-malkhut Shaddai* - to perfect this world into a kingdom of righteousness." Rather than repudiating the world, we embrace it. Rather than seeking holiness in withdrawal from life, we are commanded to invest every mundane act with holiness. Not faith, but deeds are the way to divine favor. And man needs no mediator with God. The rabbi is a man of learning and dedication, but he has no authority, privileges or obligations that put him above his congregation. These are our conceptions, our convictions. And yet, when it comes to the nitty-gritty of daily life, the attitudes and unconscious bits of behavior that make up our daily routine, which set of principles guides our actions? When we thump our Jewish hearts and content ourselves with glib affirmations of our faith, but fail to reflect these in our deeds ...

When we unthinkingly compartmentalize life into religious and secular spheres, and leave religious behind at the synagogue door at the conclusion of the service ...

When we talk easily about saintliness and spirituality and neglect the needs of our fellow man at home and abroad ...

When we ignore the needs of our children for a sound Jewish education and permit them to grow up with an infantile notion of Judaism, easy prey to every new religious faddist coming along ...

When we expect the rabbi to live our Judaism vicariously for us, to be pious for us, to keep kosher for us, to observe the holidays for us, to pray for us, or to miraculously absolve us from our sins as God's surrogate on earth ...

When we banish all Jewish thoughts from our weekday lives, reserving things Jewish for the Sabbath or the synagogue, and fail to bring Judaism into our homes ...

When we labor under the mistaken notion that Judaism is an other-worldly religion and neglect our duty to improve and enhance the world of the here and now ... then truly we tarnish our holy Torah scroll with the sign of the cross.

But this is where Rosh Hashanah comes in. For the lesson of Rosh Hashanah is that man is not doomed to inertia, that no matter how deep the pit into which we have fallen, we have the capability of reaching out to new heights. Rosh Hashanah teaches us the lesson of new beginnings, of the infinite patience of God, Who desires not the death of the sinner, but that he turn from his evil ways that he may live. Rosh Hashanah teach us that it is within our power individually and collectively to eradicate the sign of the cross that casts its baleful shadow on our faith, and to restore the Torah in our synagogue and the Torah in our hearts to its pristine beauty and purity. It is never too late – until life ceases. The initiative rests with us.

The Midrash relates that the angels inquire daily of God, "When will the new year begin?" And God replies that it is not He Who determines when Rosh Hashanah will be. "Go down to earth," He commands, "and ask My people, Israel. It is they who decide when it will be Rosh Hashanah."

The calendar, my friends, merely schedules the date of Rosh Hashanah. It is we, by our thoughts, our resolutions, our prayers, and most of all, our actions, who sanctify the day and transform it from a mere calendar listing to the Day of Judgment which marks the dawning of a new year for us and all Israel.

Let us, together, determine that our Rosh Hashanah starts here and now.

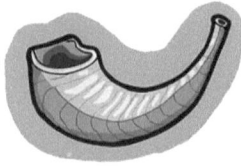

Rosh Hashanah Sermon
1979

In THE LAST 20 or 30 years a great revolution has occurred in the world. It is peculiar because we have paid little attention to it. I refer to the expansion of the size of audiences that can be reached by a program, an individual voice, or a lecture. In the past it was possible to assemble hundreds of people in an auditorium. On rare occasions it was possible to gather thousands in special facilities, as, for example in the Roman theatre in Caesarea which could hold 10,000 people, or in the Coliseum in Rome, or St. Peter's Square in the Vatican which could hold as many as 100,000 people.

But until the last several decades there was never a time when a truly vast audience of millions could be reached by one voice or one program. All of this was changed by the expansion, first of radio, and then of television broadcasting. Those of you who have occasion to travel and visit the various ends of the earth, can testify from your personal about the universal change in the skyline of cities. I am referring, not to the tall buildings and hotels that have sprung up, but to the fact that in every city, town, hamlet and village the skyline has acquired a special addition, the omnipresent television antenna. It protrudes from every roof, wherever you go. It is the visible symbol of a system of communication that can reach hundreds of millions of people at the same time. You can see the aerial on the most elegant buildings and hotels, and on the meanest huts and hovels. When you travel in the Negev desert of the land of Israel, you will see Bedouins living in the most primitive tents. Yet, on top of each tent is a television antenna. In Hong Kong you will see people so poor that they cannot even afford to live on land. They occupy miserable junks that are anchored in the harbor, and yet, their boats display the ubiquitous TV aerial. No one is beyond the reach of the electronic tube.

What is the significance of this phenomenon? Its significance lies in the fact that it has created a set of circumstances which enables most of the world to see and hear the same programs and to be exposed to the influence of ideas and concepts that, in another age, would have been limited to a very minute audience. This being the case, it is pertinent to inquire what programs have attracted the largest audiences in America and abroad in recent times. You know the answer. There were two -- they were different, but in a sense they were very much the same. The first was the series called "Roots" by Alex Haley. During the first showing, in the United States alone, it was estimated that at least 130 million people viewed it. It portrayed the story of the enslavement of the blacks and the cruel system that inhered in our country before the Civil War. The second program that had an unprecedented audience was "Holocaust," by Gerald Green. It is estimated that in the sixteen months since its premier this TV mini-series detailing the horrors perpetrated by the Nazis was viewed by more than 240 million people in 50 countries -- and this staggering number does not include the untold additional millions who watched it again or for the first time when the series was rebroadcast two weeks ago. In languages from Thai to Greek, viewers watched the unfolding drama of a Jewish family, the Weisses, most of whom were killed after the family was broken apart, and of a Nazi family, the Dorfs. By focusing on the events in the lives of the two families, the series attempts to make comprehensible the incomprehensible: the planned and systematic annihilation of European Jewry, the catastrophe in which six million of our people perished.

The effect this show has had on its audience is enormous. It stirred a debate in the German Parliament that was instrumental in that body's decision to indefinitely extend the statute of limitations for Nazi war crimes. Throughout the world it has sparked renewed interest, renewed study, renewed investigation into the phenomenon we call the Holocaust and its implications for our own times.

Both of these programs had a similar aim -- it was to reveal in dramatic form the tragic history of a specific ethnic group. To uninformed whites, the "Roots" program was a revelation. It revealed the systematic degradation of black people and the cruelty that was perpetrated upon them in our country. To uninformed gentiles, the "Holocaust" series gave the picture of the frightful epic of wholesale murder and butchery of our people. We could well anticipate the horror, shock and disbelief of those who were not fully aware of these two tragic stories. But there was also an interesting by-product of these programs that affected not those who were outsiders, but rather those who were members of these ethnic groups, the blacks and the Jews. These programs evoked a remarkable reaction from them. They became acutely aware that they have roots, that they have a history and a past that should be known and appreciated. Blacks visited libraries and went to universities to inquire about their past and their ancestry. High schools and colleges throughout the country were inundated with requests -- nay, with demands -- for black studies courses. Jews also began to ask about their grandparents and great-grandparents. A new interest in genealogy has arisen, which has not yet peaked. Since these ethnic programs were telecast Jewish institutions have been flooded with inquiries from people, many not Jews, who wanted to know where they came from. They heard that they had a Jewish past and wanted to know about it. A typical letter came from a man who was told that he was descended from Jews and he wished information about his ancestors. He signed his name John Kelly Hitchcock. He provided some clues that facilitated the search. He received an interesting answer. His great grandfather was Jewish and was named Yankele Yitzhak. It took only a few generations to transform the pronunciation of Yankele Yitzhak to John Kelly Hitchcock.

The truth of the matter is that searching for roots and knowing where you came from is an ancient Jewish idea. It is found in the Talmud; in the third chapter of Pirkei Avot. One of the greatest scholars of the first century, Akavya ben Mehallel made the following statement: "Consider three things and you will not be entrapped by sin. Know from where you came, and where you are going, and before Whom you will ultimately give a final account." What he was saying was that to make life meaningful you have to know -- where you come from, and when you know that, you must decide where you are going, and you must realize that you cannot fool yourself when you stand in the presence of God.

On Rosh Hashanah we should heed the advice of our ancient sage and ask ourselves: Where do we come from? The first step in finding yourself is to know the answer to this question. The truth of the matter is that so many of us are strangers to ourselves. The psychologists call this the crisis of identity. So many do not know who they are and where they come from. I have had this experience on any number of occasions when I served as a witness at the signing of a Ketubah, the marriage contract entered into by the groom, at his wedding, or, on sadder occasions when witnessing the writing of a Get, the bill of divorcement dissolving a marriage. For the purpose of these documents we have to know the Hebrew names of the bride and groom. We therefore ask each one: What is your Hebrew name? A frantic inquiry begins. Who remembers what Gwendolyn, or Montgomery, or Percy or Christopher are in Hebrew? Perhaps grandma or an uncle or an aunt can recall. Ultimately, they find the name, but frequently with great difficulty and after protracted searching. This forgetfulness is significant when we realize that our name is a very important part of our identity. We recall the moving scene in "Roots" where the slave owner tells the newly captured Africans that they have new names. The hero, Kunta Kinte, is told by the slaver that his name is Toby. To be sure, he asks him, "What is your name?" The slave answers, "Kunta Kinte." The master beats and whips him and asks, "What is your name?" The slave repeats, "Kunta Kinte." He refuses to give up his identity that is his name even though he is beaten to a pulp. Jewish traditions similarly tells us that one of the most important merits for which our ancestors were redeemed from Egyptian slavery was because *"lo shanu shmoteihem* - they did not change their names."

We contemporary Jews also have names and a past. Our history is replete with scholars, saints and martyrs. The story is told about Stephen Wise who was once at a reception with people of varying backgrounds. One lady was proudly boasting that her ancestors were present at the signing of the Declaration of Independence. Stephen Wise casually turned to her and said, "My ancestors were present at the giving of the Ten Commandments." We are participants in a great history. In the Dark Ages we kept the light of learning burning. We had scholars who preserved the classics not only of Jewish literature, but of Latin and Arabic literature as well. Great works of philosophy were translated from Arabic into Latin or from Latin into Arabic. In the Middle Ages when kings and princes could not read nor write, every Jewish child could read and write. We are a people who kept learning alive, who loved books and taught their children. Knowledge and culture were part of our lifeblood. We may have been poor and we may have been oppressed, but we were nourished from the roots of our tradition. A poem was written by a man who recalls the poverty of his childhood, and yet remembers how rich his life was because it was blessed with a tradition of learning and piety. For those of you who do not understand Yiddish I shall translate:

ALL I GOT WAS WORDS

When I was young and fancy free
My folks had no fine clothes for me.
All I got was words:

> *Gott tzu danken* (Thank God)
> *Gott vet geben* (God will provide)
> *Zoll men leben* and *gezunt zein*
> (May we only live and be well)

When I was wont to travel far
They couldn't provide me with a car.
All I got was words:

> *Gei gezunt* (go in good health)
> *Gei pimelekh* (go slowly)
> *Hob a gliklikhe reize* (Have a successful trip)

I wanted to increase my knowledge,
But they couldn't afford to send me to college.
All I got was words:

> *Hob seiḥel* (Have good sense)
> *Zei nisht kein naar* (Don't be foolish)
> *Torah iz die beste skhoirah* (Torah is the best
> merchandise)

The years have flown, the world has turned,
Things I've forgotten, things I've learned,
Yet I still remember:

> *Zog dem emes* (Tell the truth)
> *Gib tzedakoh* (Give charity)
> *Hob rahmonus* (Have compassion)
> *Zei a mentsh* (Be a human being)

All I got was words.

All we had was words, but they were a beautiful part of a great tradition. Even today, the search for roots is going on. It is thrilling to see what happens to our young people when they visit Israel. There you see young American high school and college students working on archeological digs, laboring in the hot sun, to unearth the history of their people. They are thrilled when they pick up a potsherd or a coin 1,800 or 2,000 years old. They are excited to find artifacts from the days of Bar Kokhva or the Maccabees and to unearth remnants of a great culture created before civilization had come to Europe. They catch a glimpse of the grandeur of Jewish history and they are proud. Bronzed from the dig they visit Yad Vashem, which houses the mementos of the Holocaust, and weep unashamedly over the destruction of a Jewish world they have never known, a world which came to an end before they were born, but with which, nevertheless, they instinctively identify: the world of their grandparents and great grandparents. They never knew where they came from.

The special insight of Akavya ben Mehallel was that if you know where you come from, it helps you to know the answer to the second question, "Where are you going?" Because so many of us are drifting, we do not have a clear perception of where we are going. I read a paragraph that was written -- believe it or not -- on a financial page. While it describes the confusion in the business world, it applies to us all, especially in the spiritual realm. The author compared us moderns to Christopher Columbus. "When he sailed, he didn't know where he was headed. When he got there, he didn't know where he was. When he left he didn't know where he had been ... And he did it all with borrowed money." Many of us are doing it exactly that way. We do not know where we come from, we do not know where we are going, and what is worse, we forget our own culture and are borrowing from other people. We feel lost and alienated. One observer said the American Jew has a one-way ticket to nowhere. It is an aimless journey heading to assimilation and to ultimate oblivion. It is the paradox of our times that we American Jews, who are so proud of the high levels our children achieve in secular learning, in colleges and in post-graduate institutions, are singularly undisturbed, perhaps even unaware, of their dismal Jewish illiteracy. There is a serious question we must ask: We have come so far. Is this the end? I ask our young people to reflect. You have a proud history going back thousands of years. Are you the last of the line? Has your family tradition come to the end of the journey as you drift with no thought of the future and no destination? If we know the heroic odyssey of our people and the past centuries that molded us, we can prepare a road map for the future.

What are the major points on that road map? There are three. One -- education - a Jew cannot be an ignoramus. We believe in knowledge and we insist that you cannot live as a Jew unless you understand what it's all about. Other religions may emphasize faith and ignore knowledge. We insist that knowledge is a prerequisite to intelligent faith. We need classes not only for our children. Adults too must study and read. Our community has many resources to offer for adult study, in congregational study groups, in the Bureau's Institute of Jewish Studies, in lectures and forums throughout the year. The magnificent library of the Hebrew Union College, the small, but excellent collection in the Bureau's Moses Zalesky Memorial Library, are there for you to use, to enjoy. There are fine books and periodicals that go unread. We must bring them into our homes. We must demonstrate to our children that we read, even as we urge them to read and to study. We must confront the scourge of television. We must reserve some time when we can talk to each other, when we can read good literature, and so begin to find and understand our roots. Education is a necessity and the mandate of this hour.

The second point on our roadmap is population. I know this is a sensitive subject with which some of you will take serious issue. We have all heard of Z.P.G., meaning Zero Population Growth. The demographers and sociologists are telling us that the world must cut down its birthrate. We are overpopulated and must hold or reduce our numbers. This may be acceptable advice to the gentiles. I am not being chauvinistic when I assert that it may be good advice for them. It is not acceptable to Jews who lost six million out of sixteen million during our lifetime. We have been cut down to a level where it is literally possible for us to become extinct as a people. Such catastrophes happened in the past, but we always recovered. In 1648 and 1649 the population of the Jews in all Europe after the Chmielnicki pogroms was cut down to an estimated one million souls. We could have been wiped out and erased from world history. Yet, after those difficult times, we increased from one million to sixteen million. We are the remnants of the pogrom which began under Hitler and which, if he had been victorious, would have destroyed us all as well. We were all under the sentence of death which would have been executed had the Nazis won the war. The truth is that we in the United States are decreasing in numbers, are already at minus Z.P.G. level. We were once three percent of the population of America. We are far less today, and we may erode to an insignificant minority if this decline continues. Our history demands an increase in population. We must not embark on a course of self-destruction. We have something of significance to give to the world. We must remain alive.

The third point on our roadmap is inspiration. We must reach the hearts of our people, especially our new young generation. We must give them a cause that will bind them to Judaism. They need spiritual excitement for great goals. It is wonderful to observe our boys and girls in our schools and our clubs. Because of the nature of my work I have frequent occasion to visit classes in the day schools, Hebrew schools and Sunday schools. They sing and dance and are happy with Jewish life, with our holidays, with their involvement with Israel, with their participation in the Jewish community through Keren Ami and through numerous projects. Yet, heartening though this experience is for the visitor, the truth is that the inspiration of the school is not enough. It is not only unfair, it is totally unrealistic to expect schools to have a lasting impact, unless the lesson the school teaches finds its counterpart in the home. Judaism never was nor can it ever be a vicarious experience. Judaism insists on personal involvement. No one can observe the *mitzvot*, study Torah, give *tzedakah*, express our concern for our fellow Jew, support our causes, and fight our battles, for us. The most important inspiration our young people need, and the only one that, in the long run, can have any permanent effect, is the positive example that we provide as parents, teachers and friends.

This is the message that comes to us on Rosh Hashanah. Akavya ben Mahallel concluded his statement with the warning: "Know before Whom you give accounting." We all stand in judgment today. Our own consciences and our hearts have to give the answer. Know where you come from. Recapture your past and be proud of it. Learn of the great contributions we have made and are still making to the world. Know where you are going. Follow an itinerary that will lead to growth and to a revival of Jewish pride and knowledge. We can do it if the message of Rosh Hashanah will penetrate our hearts. Let it remind us of our heroic past and inspire us to face a future in which young and old will march together toward a greater tomorrow for our people, for the State of Israel, and for all mankind. Amen.

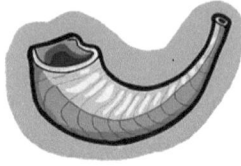

Rosh Hashanah Sermon
1980

The High Holy Days are like mountain peaks upon the landscape of the Jewish year. The rabbis describe Rosh Hashanah as a time of rebirth for the world. During these days of awe it is customary to think about the serious problems, the momentous issues, the great dilemmas of our time, the moral conflicts and challenges, by which we in this age are particularly confronted, the perennial quest for light on the meaning of life and the destiny of man. We probe the values and the goals that are worthy of a man's effort and sacrifice. We center our attention upon large problems, vast perspectives, and the fundamental thoughts with which men have grappled for many centuries.

On this first day of the present High Holy Day season, however, I would prefer to discuss the small, the apparently insignificant and trivial things, which in my opinion add up to formidable and massive obstacles on our path to a good life.

Some time ago I read of an interview with a man who had walked across the continent - one of those amazing feats of endurance with which individuals occasionally startle their fellows. He had walked from Seattle to New York. When he came to New York, he was greeted by a group of reporters. One of the questions he was asked was this: "What was it that bothered you most upon this walk from one end of the continent to the other?"

The reporters expected that he would say it was the Rocky Mountain Range, the desert, or the crowded city. This athlete, however, gave none of these answers. He said the greatest obstacle he suffered were the pebbles in his shoes. None of the large things stopped him in his tracks. The pebbles in his shoes plagued him all the way.

So it is that sometimes, as we consider large problems, we forget the pebbles in our shoes. The little deficiencies, the minor weaknesses, the small transgressions toward which we have perhaps immunized our consciences, and of which we no longer take note, these are not unimportant obstacles on the path to a better life. In The Song of Songs there is a verse about "the little foxes that despoil the vineyards." The vineyard owner did not fear the lions - he could repel them, for they made their presence known. But what of the small foxes that come in through a crack in the fence through a crevice, and despoil an entire vineyard and ruin the work and toil of many a month? They are the ones to be feared. They symbolize the little things that whittle away our spirits

Marshal Henri-Philippe Petain was a man who had served the French Republic, who had spoken in the accents of fraternity, liberty, and equality, yet he made a compact with the Nazis, the oppressors, the destroyers of civilization, and he went over to the Vichy government. When General Charles DeGaulle was asked how he explained this kind of treason, he answered, "The years had gnawed away at his character." The cause was not one momentary temptation, or the blandishment of a great reward. Petain had, in retirement, permitted the years to gnaw away at his character. When the challenge came the man was so depleted of character that he betrayed not only his own ideals, his own past, his own service, but also the Republic he served so faithfully.

It is the little foxes that we have to be concerned about. Many of us have strength enough to resist the large temptations. I do not think that any of us would ever burn anybody's house down; I do not think we would run away with anyone's funds; I do not think we would allow our hostility to drive us to violence against another. Maybe there have been moments when such things tempted us, but the fact that we are here in the synagogue rather than behind bars would indicate that at least at this point we have with some measure of success resisted these large temptations. It is the small temptations, the little hypocrisies, and the little duplicities that destroy character.

Take the matter of religion. People do not overthrow religion anymore. Religion does not go out from our lives with a huge blowout or explosion. No, we lose our religion by small leakage. Day by day, because we do not relate ourselves to it, because we allow weeks to pass without a religious thought or a religious act, it runs out in small droplets till there is nothing left; we come to the end of the year depleted. We have allowed our many, small neglects to dissolve our faith. People do not lose their faith by repudiating it all at once; they it to evaporate by small doses of abandonment. They observe religion only in high, dramatic moments, thus removing their daily lives from the domain of its influence.

What religion has to fear in our country is not dishonor. Religion is respected everywhere. I still have to hear of a candidate for office who admitted that he had not been to church recently. Indeed, the frequency with which public officials and political candidates attend religious services has worked a hardship on photographers, who must be there to photograph them in the transfigured posture of worship. No, religion will never lose out in this country for lack of respect. Nor will it lose out because of any conflict with science. We know today the limitations of science, and we know that in addition to our skill and ingenuity in exploring space and in remodeling the landscape of our life by great inventions, we need values, right attitudes, reverence, and dignity, and for these we must go to religion. Religion will lose out in America because our daily habits spring from an entirely different, almost contradictory background. Day in and day out we live in a climate of non-religion, following unreligious if not anti-religious behavior patterns. As a result, we find our religion so weakened that even when we come into high moments of prayer, the service leaves us cold. There can never be significant public worship in the total absence of private devotion, personal prayer, home worship, and the habitual cultivation of the religious spirit. And so it is with character. When we allow ourselves a little lie, when we say we're busy, or when we tell someone to answer the phone and say that we are out because we do not want to be annoyed, we are doing something that is apparently harmless. We call it a white lie. It really does not hurt anybody. But do you know what happens? We strengthen our resistance to the truth. We tell a half-truth, but a half-truth is also a half-lie. By telling it, we adjust ourselves; accommodate ourselves to the validity, to the legitimacy of lying. There was a call made upon us by an urgent communal need, and we satisfied ourselves with far less than we could give. We have an imposing array of excuses and alibis. Are others giving more? I have so many obligations. We know all the excuses, and we have begun to accustom ourselves to evading our duties. If we do this ten times or twenty times, we become utterly callous to our social responsibilities. By a series of such accommodations, we deplete our sensitivity, and lower the thresholds of obligation and compassion. The great casualty is our own character.

We are promised atonement during this season. Our tradition says, "Though your sins be as scarlet, they will become white as snow." God is a forgiving God. God will forgive our major sins. He knows how frail is the flesh, how weak and evil is the human being, how he sometimes becomes overwhelmed by a great tidal wave of temptation, and surrenders his will and judgment to his appetites. Though our sins be scarlet, vivid, bright, shining forth dramatically, they will be forgiven.

This morning, however, I worry about sins that are gray, that are not very vivid, and do not stand out like mountains - the little sins that are gray, dull, prosaic, unsensational. What of these small sins? I read of a man in the jungle who prayed, "O Lord, deliver me from the gnats - I can take care of the elephants." I think we manage well with the elephants in the jungles of our lives, but what about the little hypocrisies, the gnats of evasion, the little polite lies, the little resentments carried so long that they bring into our systems the poison of hostility? We are too civilized to go out and fight with someone, but we do nurse grudges. We nurse vindictiveness, and allow it to feed on our spirits. We nourish a little jealousy or prejudice, and it grows big enough to devour us. I am not worried about what we may do to another, but about what these little surrenders do to us, constantly weakening us, gnawing away at our characters.

A shepherd was asked how it was that sheep stray away and get lost. He answered, "They nibble themselves lost." A nibble of appetite here, a nibble of evasion there, a nibble of a lie, and we are lost. We are accustomed to think of the monumental issues of our time on the High Holy Days, to ponder once again those eternal problems of human life, to review history, and consider its large, powerful social forces.

Let us on this *Yom HaDin,* this Day of Judgment, each in the privacy of his heart and mind, think of the little foxes that destroy the vineyard, of the pebbles in our shoes, of the sheep that nibble themselves lost. By arming ourselves against these minor evasions, perhaps we shall achieve a major triumph of character and of human dignity.

Influenced by the Writings of Rabbi Morris Adler

Yom Kippur Sermon
Sowing Our Tears
Yizkor

THIS IS A SOLEMN moment in a solemn day. We pause for a moment from our regular prayers, in which we petition our Creator to grant us atonement and an extension of life, to pray for the dead, for all those who "were beloved and pleasant during their lifetime and even in their death they are not parted." We, the living, by remembering those near and dear to us who have departed from this life, bring balm and solace to their souls with the knowledge that they are not forgotten by those whom they have left behind. It is therefore appropriate that Yizkor be recited on the Day of Atonement.

There is another consideration that prompted our Sages to institute the reciting of Yizkor on Yom Kippur. Yom Kippur is a day for the shedding of tears, signifying our sincere resolve to repent of our sins and thus become worthy of God's forgiveness. "Though the gates of prayer," says the Zohar, "may at times be closed to us, the gates opened by our tears are never closed." The Talmud tells us (Shabbos 105b) that he who sheds tears over the passing away of a pious man is granted atonement for all his sins. There is a legendary cup stored in God's treasure house, and tears shed for the dead are counted and stored in this cup. The Torah reading for this Holy Day begins with a reference to the death of the two older sons of *Aharon Hakohen,* and we are assured that he who weeps over their sudden tragic death will be spared tragedy during the coming year, and the only tears he will shed will be tears of joy.

The familiar Psalm usually sung before Birkat Hamazon, which is dedicated to the time when God brings back those who return to Zion, has a poignant reference to the shedding of tears. "Those who sow in tears will reap in joy." It tells us that tears are not wasted; if sown in our hearts and minds as one sows seeds in the ground they will germinate and produce joy and satisfaction. Which generation, if not ours, can testify as readily as we can to the truth of this lesson! For generations our fathers wept over the destruction of the *Beit Hamikdash* and the dispersal of our people in *galut*. We shed tears as we read the Book of Lamentations and as we recited the *kinnot* on Tisha B'av. But the tears were not wasted; they entered our souls and kept alive our yearning for the return to Zion, making it grow into a consuming passion that finally sprouted forth in the Zionist movement, which in turn yielded the precious fruit of Jewish sovereignty in the Land of our Fathers.

In this fashion, the tears we shed on Yom Kippur as we recite the Yizkor prayer should be sown and planted in our hearts, to refresh and stimulate us to growth and development, growth as Jews understanding their Jewishness, development in our day-to-day commitment to a life of Torah and *mitzvot*. The person who honors the dead and puts it to his heart will honor the living all the more. He will be transformed by the experience of tragedy, be imbued with a keener sense and appreciation of life. He will reap in joy and find a greater happiness in closeness to the members of his family and in stronger kinship with his fellowman.

We as a people have had a common *Yom Hamitah,* a day of death for six million, a Holocaust unparalleled in our history. We remember them today; we shed tears for them and weep for the old who could not die peacefully and for the young whose lives were snuffed out so prematurely. Let us sow these tears in our hearts, freshen and strengthen our devotion to our people, so that we can reap a song of redemption, redemption from evil to righteousness, from darkness to light, from sorrow to joy, from the suffering of *galut* to the blessings of the *geulah sheleimah*. Amen.

Yom Kippur Sermon
Yizkor

THE COMPANIONSHIP OF TIME is but a short duration. It flies faster than the shades of evening. We are like a child that grasps a sunbeam. When he opens his hand he is surprised to find it empty and the brightness gone.

Today in our synagogue we join with our fellow worshippers and with our fellow Jews throughout the world in a common bond of memory. Our Yizkor services gives us the opportunity to memorialize our loved ones, to conjure up mental images of our past associations, and of what those associations have meant to us, to shed a tear for their loss, for their irreversible removal from our midst, to utter a prayer for the repose of their souls. There are those of us here today who mourn the passing of a husband or a wife, devoted partners in life, who shared our most intimate moments, our hopes and aspirations, our trials and triumphs, our good days and our bad. There are others who recall fondly the memory of a beloved brother or sister, companions of our youth with whom we shared the joys and pains of growing up, the excitement of new experiences and discoveries, the *simhas* and the sorrows of our maturity. There may be some who mourn the untimely loss of a child – torn from our midst before its promise could be fulfilled, recalled to eternity by God's inscrutable will. But most of us, at this Yizkor service, pay our respects to parents, recalling their devotion, remembering their manifold expressions of concern, their personal achievements and their aspirations for their children. We evoke their memory in gratitude, not only for the physical life which they bestowed upon us, but as well for the legacy of heart and spirit, of ideals and convictions, of moral teachings and Jewish commitments with which they raised and molded us, with which they endowed us and challenged us.

We honor their memory, not as some form of ancestor worship, not in a maudlin spirit of sentimentality, nor to storm heaven with recriminations, but rather that their memory serve to inspire us, the living, to better living; that the example of their lives, of their ideals, might awaken an echo in our hearts and bestir us to greater efforts toward reaching our potential.

The Yizkor is neither a mournful dirge nor a lament over the finality of death. We accept death, for we know that we are mortal, that we are born to die. Our tradition tells us that, *"ke-sheim she-me-varkhim al ha-tovah kakh me-varkhim al ha-ra'ah* - We must take the bad with the good and bless God's holy Name." "*Hashem natan ve-Hashem lakah, yehi shem Hashem mevorakh* - God has given and God has taken away, may the name of God be blessed." The Yizkor, rather, is an affirmation of life everlasting, a declaration that love and ideals transcend the grave. The Yizkor brings us to an awareness that though life is finite, the quality of life is infinite; that though medicine can add years to our lives, only our resolve and our convictions can add life to our years. When life is filled with striving and achieving, with love of God and *ma'asim tovim,* when generations pass on these ideals and these concerns to children and friends so that they become an integral part of their lives in turn, then death is not an ending, but only a shifting of the burdens and opportunities of life – *Ve-yitzror be-tzror ha-hayim et nishmatam* – then the lives of those we have lost are bound up in the eternal bond of life with the ancestors that have preceded them and with the generations yet to follow. They are not dead who live on in our hearts. They are not dead who live on in their works. They are not dead who live on in their children. The Apocrypha tells us in the second Book of Baruch that, "With the Most High, account is not taken of much time or a few years. What did it profit Adam that he lived nine hundred and thirty years, and transgressed? … Or wherein did Moses lose by living only 120 years though privileged to light a lamp for the nation of Israel." We are all familiar with great men and women, whose lives flashed like a streak of lightning across the horizon of human experience, flashed and were gone, but in that short flash illuminated and changed the world into which they were born. Conquerors of the ancient world like Alexander the Great and Julius Caesar, philosophers like Aristotle, composers like Mozart, painters like Van Gogh, patriots like Nathan Hale, dreamers in Zion like Theodore Herzl – the list could go on and on – lived but briefly, but oh, how they changed the world.

Not everyone can be a conqueror, or a sage or an artist, but there is within each of us, and there was in each of those whom we recall today, a special quality, a special legacy with which we enrich the world. It is for this quality, for what we bring to life, not for the number of our years that we will be remembered.

The Yizkor teaches us that though life is fleeting, it is precious. Knowing life's brevity, we the living are reminded to use our time wisely, to treasure our families, our friends, while we can, to make our contribution to our people and our society while we can, to raise our children that they will want to recall us as we recall our parents today, to make sure that our lives count, while yet we may be counted among the living. The Yizkor service bids us to reflect. In the words of the prayer book, *"Mah anu, mah hayeinu, mah hasdeinu, mah tzidkoteinu, mah yeshuateinu, mah koheinu, mah g'vurateinu* – What are we? What is our life? What is our goodness? What is our virtue? What our help? What our strength? What our might?"

And to respond that our life can have meaning and purpose, that our existence may be a source of blessing to the generations to come and a source of credit to the forebears from whom we derive, that we have it in our means to endow life with quality and with significance. With the psalmist we pray, *"Limnot yameinu kein hodah, ve navi levav hokhma* – Teach us to number our days that we may get us a heart of wisdom."

The Talmud relates the story of Honi, who one day saw a farmer planting a carob tree. "Why do you trouble to plant this tree?" he asked Honi. "What is the purpose of your labors? Know you not that this tree will not bear fruit for seventy years? Do you expect to live seventy more years, old as you are, to eat of its fruit?" Replied the farmer, "The world into which I was born contained carob trees my parents planted for me. I plant now for my children."

My friends, our world contains many carob trees – many good things that our parents, our loved ones toiled over, nurtured and bequeathed to us. We will honor their memory best, we will add our years of life to theirs best, we will make of our lives a worthy link of the *tzror ha-hayim* in which we ask God today to bind up their lives, if we heed the farmer's sage answer. Let us plant as our parents have planted. Let us endow our lives with high purpose and noble achievements, that succeeding generations will say of us, their lives mattered; they are alive today, for their works live after them. Amen.

Yom Kippur Sermon
1973

THERE ARE MANY THINGS we could talk about this evening. We could make some comments on the significance of Kol Nidre as a means of wiping the slate clean, of giving us a fresh new start, uncluttered with carried-over unfulfilled obligations from the past year. Or, we could profitably explore the concepts of *Bein Adam Le-Makom* (the nature of our relationship and the obligation implied in our relationship with God), and *Bein Adam Le-haveiro* (the nature of our interaction with our fellow human beings), and the obligations that they impose upon us as Jews and as human beings living in a free society.

Though nearly 30 years have passed since the agony and horror of the decimation of our people in the European Holocaust, historians and theologians are still grasping for answers to the unanswerable questions: Why? How could God let this scourge be unleashed against His people? A discussion on this subject would not be inappropriate on this evening of solemn reflection. Or we could talk about current events and trends in Jewish life and their import to Israel and the Diaspora, of Soviet Jewry and its aspirations, of the search for Jewish identity, of the material and human tragedy of the 25 years of war plaguing our brethren in Israel – a war that continues unabated with no prospects of the long yearned for peace in sight.

We could talk of all of these, and of many other things beside. But I have chosen to speak to you this evening on a topic that is of vital and immediate concern to me as a Jewish educator, and that should be of consequence to all of us who take ourselves seriously as Jews. I am referring to the regeneration gap crisis that threatens the future of Jewish life in our community, as it does to other communities the length and breadth of our country. Now, I hope you heard me correctly. I did not say "generation gap." I said "regeneration gap." The two are not the same. Though people have been wringing their hands for the past number of years over the "generation gap," it is not this which I believe to be the major problem. Our problem is not the gap between the generations, but the gap between what is and what is necessary to regenerate creative and vibrant Jewish life in America in general, and in Cincinnati in particular. Permit me to digress for a minute. Personally, I like a bit of a generation gap. Perhaps I'm old-fashioned, but I don't approve of the breakdown in traditional courtesies expressed by the younger generation to the older, in the supposed spirit of better communication, greater spontaneity, and equality without regard to age. I don't approve of the *mishegas* of children addressing parents and teachers by their first names, of parents trying to be "buddies" to their children rather than parents, of children contradicting their parents publicly and often disrespectfully, of the neglect and disappearance of courtesy shown to one's elders.

Jewish tradition, from our earliest period to fairly recent times is replete with aphorisms that stress the respect due to age, and with tales of filial respect and deference. Our Torah teaches us, *"Kabeid et avikha ve-et imekha* - Honor thy father and thy mother," *"Lifnei seiva takum* - Rise before your elders," and *"Ve-hadarta penei zaken* - Treat your elders respectfully."

Even the non-Jewish world until recent times enjoyed this kind of positive generation gap - courtesy to one's elders, teachers and parents; rising when one's parent or teacher entered the room; offering a seat on the bus to one's elders; deferring to experience (at least not publicly contradicting) of one's parents; speaking when spoken to; and so forth.

But it's not this positive type of generation gap we've been hearing about for the past number of years. What has been drummed into our ears is that there has been a nearly total breakdown of communications between the generations, and that this is the cause for nearly all that ails society, or at least its younger members, today. From lack of manners to disrespect of authority, to dishonesty, to shoplifting, to juvenile delinquency, from drugs to promiscuity, all is due – we are told – to the generation gap.

In the Jewish community it's more of the same, but slanted to Jewish *tzores*. Jewish youth is alienated from its Jewish moorings – generation gap. Jewish youth rejects our time-honored values, religious forms and practices – generation gap. Our young people are marrying outside the faith in alarming numbers – generation gap. Jewish youth is the vanguard of radical movements to the detriment of Jewish causes – generation gap. The stability of the Jewish home is gone and the divorce rate of newly married couples is beginning to approximate the marriage rate – generation gap.

I would like to suggest to you that this is rubbish. Anyone who thinks that this is really the problem is deluding himself. We are not experiencing any generation gap. On the contrary, we are witnessing today a greater fidelity by our children to the things the adult world stands for, as exemplified by its daily acts of omission and commission, than ever before. Far from kicking over the traces, from rejecting the adult world, our children are a mirror of ourselves, giving us back in spades what we have taught them of our values by our actions. We may kid ourselves as to our values, we may preach all kinds of pious platitudes, but we don't fool anyone – certainly not our children. They don't do as we say or pontificate. They do as we do!

Generation gap? Where did our children learn dishonesty, discourtesy, immorality, promiscuity, drug culture, if not from the adult world? Our adult culture – the world of business, and of government, of industry and of commerce, of mass media and of politics – is not known for its high moral fiber. It has brought cheating, dishonesty and immorality to new abysmal depths. What lessons impress themselves on the minds of our youth about our adult values when national and local leaders of business and government, men at the pinnacle of their professional, esteemed by their fellows, from local judiciary to the attorney general of the United States, from presidents of giant corporations to the official family of the president of the U.S., stand exposed as liars and cheats, as morally and financially corrupt? Our mass media pill pushers have brain washed an entire generation that there's a pill for everything that ails us. Small wonder our kids are receptive to the blandishments of the drug pusher. Big business flaunts sex – the rawer the better – to sell every conceivable product, makes the smut movies that glut our theaters, publishes the slick magazines and pornographic books that besmirch our newsstands, floods the market with worthless products – all the time posturing with pious platitudes.

And let's not forget the example we all too often set for our children ourselves, examples of intolerance and prejudice, of dishonesty and discourtesy, of disrespect and self-seeking.

Turning to Jewish concerns, I am often puzzled by the hand wringing of parents whose homes are totally devoid of Jewish content, over their children's alienation from Judaism. No generation gap, there. Their children are giving them the greatest compliment – by imitating them.

When parents don't read Jewish books, don't attend services, don't aspire to any Jewish knowledge, don't observe Jewish law and ritual, don't cultivate Jewish associations, don't move in Jewish circles, turn Judaism into some kind of anachronistic fossil, and equate Judaism with nothing more than a vague humanism, or a twinge in the pocketbook during the annual Jewish Welfare Fund Drive, or even less, what standards of Jewish loyalty can they anticipate from their children?

Who has taught our children that Jewish learning and the Jewish school are really unimportant, not to be taken seriously, if not the Jewish parent? When little leagues, the swim team, the bowling team, the Bengals and the Reds come before Hebrew School, what do we convey to our children of our sense of values? What are we teaching our children about the importance of Jewish scholarship when we demand excellence in general studies, are unhappy unless our children rate admission to Walnut Hills High School, work with them, engage tutors for them to get them over the rough spots in their secular studies, and then berate the religious school teacher the minute the children experience difficulties in their Jewish studies, or better yet, pull them out of religious school because, "the teachers are not good," "they don't learn anything," or "he can't cope with the double program"? When the college degree in secular studies is becoming a commonplace, but we begrudge our children the time for a one-day-a-week, or a three-day-a-week, or even a day school education beyond the elementary years, what do we teach our children about our attitude to Jewish life? No, my friends, not a generation gap, but a regeneration gap confronts us. Judaism through the centuries has faced oblivion many times. It has undergone, in many periods and in many climes, some of the very problems which confront us today – assimilation, decline in scholarship, diminution in numbers, and the lure of the outside world. Each time we survived and went on to new heights of achievement through a process of regeneration, of rising from the ashes, of rebuilding the institutions and the forms which gave our people their uniqueness and their sense of purpose.

Webster's defines "regenerate" as 1. to become formed again, 2. to change radically for the better, 3. to generate or produce anew, 4. to restore to original strength or properties, 5. to subject to spiritual regeneration.

The gap that exists between the ideal to which we aspire and the actual in which we wallow, is the regeneration gap that concerns me, that concerns all who value the continuity of Jewish life in America. Judaism must be regenerated in the sense of all of Webster's definitions, if it is to be a real force in the shaping of our existence. It must become formed again, changing radically for the better, producing anew, restoring original strength or properties, and be subject to spiritual regeneration. And in this process of regeneration there can be no generation gap. When God commanded Abraham to offer his son as a sacrifice on Mount Moriah, the Torah tells us, *"Va-yeilkhu shneihem yahdav* - Father and son, both went together" – united in purpose and united in the determination to do God's will. When Pharaoh asked Moses whom it was that he wanted to take into the wilderness to hold a feast unto the Lord, Moses' answer was very concise and clear, *"be-na'areinu u-vizkeineinu neilekh* - We will go with our young and our old." In matters of the spirit, in matters of the Jewish will to be, in the regeneration of the sources of our strength, we must go with our young and our old – father and son together.

Such a process of regeneration must put Jewish learning and Jewish piety into a position of respect and prominence in our daily lives. Jewish action and Jewish knowledge and Jewish survival are inextricably bound together. For our children and ourselves this means strengthening and enriching the goals and structure of Jewish education.

It has become fashionable in some circles to speak of the failure of Jewish education. This is absurd. Jewish education has not failed where it has been applied assiduously. The graduates of Yeshiva University, of Torah Vodaath, of Ner Israel, of Telz, and of Chaim Berlin, of the many fine institutions that dot our country, bear ample witness to this truth. What has gone wrong is that we have used the label of Jewish education too loosely – that we have deluded ourselves into thinking that four or five years of 3 hours or 7 hours-a-week, constitute the sum total of Jewish education necessary for a meaningful Jewish life. Small wonder our children view Judaism in infantile terms, and reject it when they reach maturity.

Even our day schools, excellent as they are, cannot be expected to produce lifelong results. A total Jewish education, just as a total secular education, must reach into the high school years and beyond. It is time we dropped the double standard when it comes to Jewish education. If we are to close the regeneration gap in Cincinnati, a first prerequisite is the establishment of a secondary day school to build on the solid foundations laid at Yavneh and Hebrew Day School. If we are to close the regeneration gap, we must see to it that even greater numbers of our children receive the advantages of a day school education that prides itself on dual excellence, excellence in secular studies as well as in Judaica.

If we are to close the regeneration gap, we must emulate the example of the great sage Rabbi Akiva, who began his studies at the age of 40 and became the greatest sage in the annals of Judaism. The Ethics of the Fathers tells us, *"Ein bor yirei het ve lo am ha-aretz hasid* - An empty headed man cannot be a sin fearing man, nor can an ignorant person be truly pious." Regeneration cannot be accomplished in the face of wide spread ignorance on the part of our adult community. The demands we make on our children are demands we should make equally upon ourselves. There are ample opportunities for adult study. Would that more adults took advantage of them!

Regeneration demands of us a return to Jewish practices, setting an example to our children of Jewish living in its fullest sense. The synagogue must become more than a three day-a-year prayer hall, the Jewish library more than a mausoleum for dead and forgotten books, the Jewish home more than a museum of Jewish artifacts and unused prayer books.

There is a term you have heard often during these High Holy Days. That term is *teshuvah,* penitence – returning to God. What is regeneration if not *teshuvah,* a return to God. As the *Aseret Yamei Teshuvah* come to an end today and tomorrow, let us then reflect on ways in which we can close the regeneration gap, that we may confidently look forward to the day of which the prophet spoke long ago – a day without a generation gap – a day when *"Heishiv lev avot al banim ve-lev banim al avotam* - He shall turn the hearts of the fathers to the children and the heart of the children to the fathers." And let that day speedily come. Amen.

Yom Kippur Sermon
1974

WITH THE KOL NIDRE services this evening, we usher in the sacred Day of Atonement, culminating the ten days of reflection and penitence that we began on Rosh Hashanah. These were days for spiritual stocktaking, for examining our achievements and our shortcomings, and for resolving to strengthen the good and eliminate the bad. Our sages were wise, indeed, in instituting this annual custom of *heshbon ha-nefesh*. It is a wholesome and healthy practice for each person to pause from time to time to ponder over where we are and where we are going. I trust that we have, all of us, profited from the introspection of the past days, and have emerged from the process of reflection of strengthened in our good resolves and reinvigorated in our noble purposes.

But, beyond the individual stocktaking, perhaps this Kol Nidre evening would also be a good time to take a look at ourselves collectively, to see where American Jewry as a whole is, and where we are headed. As American Jews we have notably been concerned with the welfare of Jewish communities throughout the world. Are we equally concerned with our own future?

On September 4th, there appeared a full-page advertisement in the New York Times, which on succeeding days was published by Newsday, an assortment of New York and Long Island newspapers, and several Anglo-Jewish papers as well. The ad read as follows: "If You're Jewish, Chances Are Your Grandchildren Won't be." I repeat, "If You're Jewish,

Chances Are Your Children Won't be." That's right – plain and simple – an ever increasing rate of intermarriage, assimilation, alienation from Judaism, and a lack of Jewish education is resulting in a decline of American Jewry. Current trends indicate that in a matter of time there will be no American Jewry to speak of. Finish. No more.

"A substantial number of today's Jewish population is being raised without any knowledge of the history, culture and traditions of the Jewish people. And their children, your grandchildren, will probably be brought up without any Jewish thought – in essence, lost to the Jewish way of life. No Jewish faith. No Jewish culture. No Jewish beliefs. And no Jewish life experiences." This advertisement was followed in succeeding days by another full-page ad that read as follows: "What Happened to the Jews in Europe in 1939 the Jews are Doing to Themselves in 1974. In 1939, the anti-Semitic current in Europe attempted to strip the Jew of his heritage. Everything held precious: his books, his education, his art, his way of life --- destroyed. Then came the Holocaust and the end of six million. In America the same thing is happening --- only this time, we're doing it to ourselves. Today there are six million Jews in America and that figure is dwindling. The rate of intermarriage is 31.7%. The rates of conversion, assimilation, and alienation from Judaism are reaching frightening proportions. And it means, in a matter of time, there won't be an American Jewry to speak of." Those are strong words that conjure up an unbelievable prospect: the prospect of American Jewry, without any doubt the strongest, most affluent and most secure community of Jews the world has ever known, phasing itself out of existence within the next two generations. We'd like to challenge the allegations of the ads. We find its basic premise repugnant. Surely the ads were placed by some irresponsible crackpot fundamentalist whose scare tactics we should disavow and whose simplistic approach to Jewish life in the 20th century is out of touch with reality! But no, my friends. The ads, and the posters, radio spots, and direct mail campaign that accompanied them, were not the work of a crackpot alarmist, but rather that of a very conservative and responsible group of people who concerned over the decline in the quality of Jewish life in America, felt and impelling need to sound a warning. With the unifying theme of Survival Through Education, this was an effort undertaken by the Board of Jewish Education of New York, financed by a $50,000 grant from the Federation of Jewish Philanthropies of New York whom no one will accuse of radical irresponsibility, a full year in discussion and preparation, to try to rouse out of their lethargy the parents of the many thousands of Jewish children in New York who are not receiving any Jewish education whatsoever. The statistics they referred to were not the imaginings of a mind run amok, but the carefully researched scholarly conclusions of the National Jewish Population Study sponsored by the Council of Jewish Federations and Welfare Funds and reported in Volume 74 of the American Jewish Yearbook published by the American Jewish Committee and the Jewish Publications Society of America.

The stark, challenging words of the advertisements may impel us to a spirited disavowal of the allegations. We look about and see the imposing structures we have reared -- Jewish universities, houses of worship that vie with Christian cathedrals for magnificence, hospitals and Centers with tennis courts and swimming pools, institutions great and small, and we're inclined to scoff at the alarmists. Is Jewry in America on the decline? Never! And yet, deep down in our hearts we know that they speak the truth. For the fact is that while we have been raising unprecedented millions for the preservation of Judaism in all parts of the world, and while we have lavished additional untold millions to satisfy the edifice complex at home, we have been unmindful of the deterioration of the quality of Jewish life and the precipitous decline in Jewish awareness in our own backyard. While we have been busy sounding the alarm for Israel and Soviet Jewry, we're paid scant attention to the voices that have been raised on the deplorable status of American Judaism. Some years ago it was fashionable to picture Jewish education in America as a river -- a mile wide -- covering a vast landscape of Jewish knowledge and lore -- but only an inch deep -- contenting itself with minimal achievements and very shallow levels of Jewish learning. Today this description may be even more applicable to Jewish life in America in general, for while we have no shortage of Jewish organizations and of Jewish activities, the quality of Jewishness in these organizations and the level of Jewishness in these endeavors are exceedingly shallow. Our organizations are efficient fundraisers, adept at social gatherings, proficient in the superficialities of Jewish life. But when it comes to *takhlis*, to any real depth of Jewishness in program, involvement of commitment, our organized Jewish community leaves much to be desired.

We don't really need the statisticians and the researchers to tell us about the current status of American Judaism, and the real danger of its rushing headlong into oblivion. We need only open our eyes and look around.

The Hebrew word *kadosh* means holy. We find this word in its innumerable permutations from *kaddish* to *kiddush,* from *kedushah* to *mekadesh,* throughout our prayer books, daily and Sabbath as well as High Holy Days.

But the basic meaning of *kadosh* is set apart, unique. Thus, the Jewish people, throughout our history, were referred to as a *goy kadosh,* a holy people, a unique people, a people apart. We prided ourselves on our uniqueness. We were the chosen people, the people selected by God to carry the message of His Torah to an unbelieving world. We were unique in the strength of the home and the strong closely knit family unit. We were unique in our fidelity to the marriage bonds. We were unique in our conception of righteousness and our pursuit of social justice. We were unique in our concern for each other, for the weak and the poor, for the sick and the weary, for the stranger and the wayfarer. We were unique in our love for learning and thirst for knowledge. We were unique in our emphasis on the spiritual and the moral over the physical and the material. We were unique in clinging to God's commands, not as a literary selection from the Bible to be memorized, but as a living force in our daily lives. When we recited in our *brakhot* the words *asher kideshanu be-mitzvotav,* they inspired not only that God sanctified us by His commandments, but also that by observing His commands we achieved the status of *goy kadosh,* of a unique, a consecrated people.

When the walls of the ghetto began to crack and crumble during the early years of the 19th century, Jews were confronted by the problem that their admission to Western society often came at the price of shedding their Jewish uniqueness. To be different was opprobrium. To be a Frenchman, to be a German, to be English, meant to shed one's veneer of Jewish uniqueness, to be like everyone else. And yet, though anxious to enter the mainstream of Western culture, this price to many seemed too steep. This tension between wanting to be Jews and yet wanting to be like everyone else, to be different, but not so as you could tell, has been with us ever since. But in the last few decades, in America in particular, the process of acculturation and assimilation, of shedding the garb of Jewishness and blending indistinguishably into the general culture, has accelerated to the point where it threatens our survival as an identifiable religious and cultural entity. Are we still a *goy kadosh,* a unique people? Unless we act forcefully now, can we remain a *goy kadosh* in the years and generations ahead?

To an even greater extent we have lost and are losing those traits and characteristics as a people that have been the tokens of our uniqueness. Our solidarity as a people is threatened by the spiraling rate of intermarriage. 31.7% of all Jewish persons married between 1966-1972 married outside the faith. 9.2% of all Jews who are married today have non-Jewish spouses. The stability of the Jewish home is a thing of the past. The divorce rate, in the past only a fraction of the divorce rate in the non-Jewish world, is climbing at an unprecedented pace, equal to our gentile neighbors. The virtues that characterized the Jewish home: modesty, chastity, respect for parents and elders, ritual observances, study, self-discipline, have been sadly impaired in an ever-rising number of Jewish homes. Today we have our share and more of broken homes, of promiscuity and delinquency, of school dropouts, of drug addicts, of police records. In abandoning our Jewish uniqueness, our youth, all too often, has been attracted to the seamy, rather than the healthy side of the general culture. From being an *Am Ha-Sefer,* a People of the Book, we are rapidly becoming Jewish illiterates. Only in our concern for our fellow Jew, in our philanthropic and altruistic efforts on behalf of our people, wherever they may be, do we fully live up to the traditions of a *goy kadosh,* of a unique people.

What oppression and persecution, from Haman to Hitler, failed to achieve, apathy and ignorance are bringing about. For the most serious threat to our survival is not only that our children don't care. It is that our children don't know! Far from making their choice between acceptance or rejection of Judaism on the basis of a clear-cut understanding of the alternatives, they are in increasing numbers rejecting a Judaism they know nothing about, and turning for their inspiration to Jesus Freaks, to esoteric Eastern cults, or simply to hedonistic pursuits.

We have been most remiss in fulfilling the responsibility of parenthood that we recite in the Shema, *"Ve-shinantem le-vanekha -* And you shall teach them diligently unto your children." The fact is that American Jewry has been far from diligent in its instruction of its children.

In New York it is estimated that over 100,000 children out of the 400,000 children in school age are not enrolled in any Jewish school. The numbers in Cincinnati are obviously much smaller, but the ratio may not be much different – one out of every four Jewish children receives absolutely no Jewish education. Equally serious is the quality and quantity of instruction for children who are enrolled in Jewish schools at some point. The majority of our children are withdrawn from our school after Bar Mitzvah, precisely at the point where meaningful instruction can begin. No wonder that as adults they turn their backs on a Judaism that seems infantile to them. For Judaism is not a pediatric religion. The truths of our faith, the literature and history of our people, the accumulated wisdom of our heritage, are not for children.

But we must not succumb to despair. If the High Holy Days teach us anything at all, it is that there is always an opportunity for a new beginning. The prayer book reminds us, *"Ne'um Adonai Elohim, im ehpotz be-mot ha-rasha, ki im be-shuv rasha mi-darko, ve-hayah* – So says the Lord God, I have no pleasure in the death of the wicked, but that the wicked turn from his way and live." American Jewry need not fade into oblivion. We may yet turn back from the road to nowhere, and find our way to the road of Jewish survival in America.

There is an antidote to apathy, and that is self-awareness. There is an antidote to ignorance, and that is study. If we can break through the barrier of apathy to a self-awareness of who and what we are, if we can strengthen our schools, enhance our educational programs, and take the role of our school seriously, if we can see to it that <u>all</u> of our children will receive instruction, then we can yet reverse the tide of assimilation and alienation.

If we are not to recite a new *Al Het,* a new confessional for the sins we have committed by our acquiescence to the eradication of Jewish life in America, then on this Kol Nidre evening, when we ask God to release us of old vows we have not fulfilled, we must at the same time resolve to undertake new vows, and do our best to live up to them. We must vow to do all we can to strengthen Jewish education in America, by raising the standards of support for Jewish schools, by demanding quality education of our schools, and by staffing our schools with teachers who are knowledgeable in subject matter and competent in teaching techniques. We must vow to do our utmost to give our own children a thorough Jewish education, an education that goes beyond the elementary school into the high school years and adult life.

We must vow to influence our neighbors and friends to do likewise. We must vow to demonstrate to our children in every way we can that what they learn in the Jewish school matters to us. And finally, we must vow to set a personal example for our children, by our own participation in Jewish study, and by enhancing our own knowledge and appreciation of our Jewish heritage. "Jewish parents who fail to enroll their children in a Jewish school are helping to sign a death sentence for American Jewry," says Dr. Alvin I. Schiff, Executive Vice President of the Board of Jewish Education in New York. Let us by our resolves and actions show that as a people, as well as individuals, we want to live. Let us strive to become again a *goy kadosh,* a unique people, a people set apart by our ideals and our way of life, a people whose roots are anchored in the dim past and whose future extends to the end of time.

Yom Kippur Sermon
1975

ONE OF THE MOST prominent features of the Yom Kippur liturgy is the recitation of the *Al Het*, the public confession of sins. Before the shofar is sounded tomorrow evening to announce the conclusion of the Day of Atonement, we will have repeated this listing of some fifty-four sins to which we individually and collectively confess, ten times. What are the sins for which we ask God's forgiveness? You would expect that on Yom Kippur, seeking a return to God, we would acknowledge our lapses of faith, our heretical thoughts, our failure to properly observe Shabbos and *Yom Tov* and *kashrus*, and all of the other minutiae of Jewish law which, in their totality, compose the Jewish way of life. What the rabbis called the *"Mitzvot Bein Adam Le-Makom* - our obligations to God." But this is not the case. The *Al Het* does not concern itself at all with doctrines or observances, with the ritual or theological aspects of our faith. Rather, it directs itself to the stuff of daily life, to our shortcomings in the social sphere *Bein Adam Le-haveiro*, in our day-to-day relationships with our fellow man. It points an accusing finger at our moral failures. In *Al Het* we express our contrition for pride, callousness, insolence, wanton hatred, envy, slander, corrupt business practices, deceit, disrespect toward parents and teachers, and the corruption of justice. One is struck, in particular, in reading through this listing of our avowed shortcomings, at the large number of sins that are related not so much to what we do as to what we say. Our society is an action-oriented society. We tend to think of sin, if we think of sin at all, in terms of things that people do, not in terms of what people say. Stealing, robbing, killing, those are surely sins. But talking, just talking, what can be wrong with that? We've grown up with the nursery jingle that "sticks and stones can break my bones, but names can never hurt me." What is the *Al Het* trying to tell us? The Midrash relates the story of Rabbi Simeon ben Gamliel, the great sage, Head of the Sanhedrin, who one day sent his servant Tabbi to the market place to buy the finest cut of meat he could find. Shortly the servant returned and brought him a tongue. Some days later Rabbi Simeon sent Tabbi to the market again, this time instructing him to secure the poorest cut of meat. Again Tabbi returned bearing tongue. "How is it that when I asked you to fetch me the finest cut of meat you brought tongue, yet now that I instructed you to get the poorest cut, you bring me tongue again?" Replied the wise servant, "Both good and evil are in the tongue. If it is good, there is nothing better; and if it is bad, there is nothing worse."

The tongue - the faculty of speech - the power of language – is one of the distinguishing characteristics of mankind that sets us apart from all of God's creations. But it is the use to which we put this gift that renders it a blessing or a curse.

With deep insight the Bible tells us, in Proverbs 18:21, *"Mavet ve-hayim be-yad lashon* - death and life are in the power of the tongue." And again in Psalms 34:13-14, *"Mi ha-ish he-hafetz hayim oheiv yamim lirot tov* - Who is the man that desires life and loves days that he may see good therein? *Netzor le-shonkha me-rah u-sefatekha me-dabeir mirmah* - Keep thy tongue from evil and thy lips from speaking guile."

The faculty of speech can be a powerful force for good or a devastating drive to evil. It can transmit goodly heritage, or preach a doctrine of hate; it speaks with sacred tongue of the prophets, or with the demonical frenzy of a Hitler. It is the tool of poetry and philosophy that brighten our lives, the song of love and friendship that invest life with meaning, or the howling of the ravening mob, the cutting epithet shouted in defiance.

How do we use our faculty for speech? Do we use it as did Aaron the High Priest, whom Hillel bids us to emulate in Pirkei Avot as an *"oheiv shalom v'rodef shalom, oheiv et ha-briyot u-mekorvan le-torah* - a man who loved peace and actively pursued it, loving his fellow creatures and drawing them near unto the Torah." Aaron was the great peacemaker in rabbinic legend. He would, in the case of an open rupture between two men, hasten first to one, then to the other, saying to each, "If thou dids't but know how he with whom thou hast quarreled regrets his hard words to thee!" With the result that the former enemies would in their hearts forgive each other, and as soon as they were again face-to-face, would great each other as friends. His kindness led many a man who was about to commit a sin, to say to himself, "How shall I be able to face Aaron?" Thus did Aaron turn way many from iniquity. Or do we employ our faculty of speech to drive a wedge between friends, to spread juicy gossip, to insinuate, to malign, to slander, and to bear malicious tales? The Talmud early took note of the destroying potential of character assassination by classing such behavior as the equivalent of murder. Do we indulge in the cutting remark to wife or husband, the short-tempered disparagement or our children or our employees? Do we weigh our words and their effect before we speak? How many times have we wished for the power to recall the thoughtless word, the bitter phrase? We observe with Ibn Gabriol, "Before I speak I am master of the word; after I speak the word is master of me."

"Al het shehatanu le-fanekha be-dibur peh - For the sin we committed in Thy sight by offensive speech." One cannot love the Creator, if one has no regard for His creations. Our callousness, our moral shortcomings, our offenses against our fellow man, are offenses against God Himself. In tomorrow's Haftarah the prophet Isaiah thunders against those who content themselves with perfunctory performance of ritual practices. "Can such be my chosen fast, the day of man's self-denial? To bow down his head like a bulrush, to sit in sackcloth and ashes? ... Is that what you call fasting, a day acceptable to the Lord? Behold, this is the fast that I esteem precious ... If you remove from your midst the yoke of oppression, the finger of scorn and the speaking of malice, if you put forth your soul to the hungry, and satisfy the wretched, then shall your light rise in darkness and be bright as noon."

On this Kol Nidre night, then, as we stand before Almighty God, confessing our sins and seeking reconciliation through *teshuvah*, true and contrite repentance, we pray, *"Elohai netzor le-shoni mei'ra u-sefati me-dabeir mirmah* - Lord, Guard our tongues from evil and our lips from speaking guile." We are ashamed of our collective failings. Who among us has not indulged, at one time or another, in idle gossip, in offensive speech, in vulgarity and dishonesty, in slander and in insolence, in swearing falsely and in blasphemous utterances, in insincere fawning and in malicious tale-bearing? Not only are these heinous sins in themselves, but by inciting us and those around us to actions that so often grow out of words, their damaging influence is multiplied many times, one sin bringing another in its train.

May we go forth from this House of God cleansed of our sins and resolved to sin no more: to use our faculty of speech for good and for a blessing, for the service of mankind, and thus for the service of God; to speak kindly to our fellow man and of our fellow man.

May we find our portion among the disciples of Aaron, *"oheiv shalom u-rodef shalom, oheiv et ha-briyot u-mekorban le torah* - loving and pursuing peace, loving our fellow creatures and through our actions and our words drawing them near to Torah." Verily, *"Mavet ve-hayim be-yad lashon* - Death and life are in the power of the tongue." May we be granted the wisdom to choose life. Amen.

Yom Kippur Sermon
1976

LADIES AND GENTLEMEN, THIS past summer I had the *zekhut* to visit Israel for the first time. Those of you who have had this experience know without my attempting to define it for you, my feelings as I stepped off the plane at Ben-Gurion airport. Those of you who have yet to experience this unforgettable thrill – there's no way to put it into words for you. When you go for yourselves – and I hope you will go, and soon – you will undoubtedly feel the same upsurge of emotions, the same heightening of expectations, the same sense of exhilaration that I felt at that moment.

Because in stepping on the soil of Israel – the first independent Jewish state in two millennia – we can truly say *Shehehiyanu,* for the privilege of being members of a generation blessed with the miracle of Israel's rebirth. And truly, Israel's whole history, from the reestablishment of the state 28 years ago to its present struggle for survival can only be seen in miraculous terms.

And this miracle, which is Israel, has from its inception had three partners – God, whose Divine providence is evident in every aspect of Israel's ability to withstand the military prowess and the massed hatred of the Arab world and its vassals in the Third World, the Communist world, and even the Western world; the people of Israel whose resourcefulness and determination, sacrifice and bravery, pioneering in the physical, social and moral areas of life have set an example unmatched by any people in human history; and the Jewish people of the world, whose support, moral, spiritual, and financial have enabled Israel to face its enemies with confidence in her ability to survive and flourish.

This three-fold partnership is being called on again to produce a new miracle in Israel's present economic plight – a battle for survival no less urgent and pressing than the Yom Kippur War three years ago.

I'm not concerned with the first two partners to this ongoing miracle of Israel. God will not forsake His people, and the people of Israel, long-conditioned to sacrifice and self-denial, will continue their heroic efforts on the economic front as they have on the military battle fronts of four wars.

What about us, the third partner to the miracle? On this eve of Yom Kippur, when our fate is to be sealed for the coming year, will we be found wanting?

In lieu of a Kol Nidre sermon, I have been asked to bring the following message to you from Israel Bonds. Please give it your full attention and respond commensurate to the need.

1. GENERAL INTRODUCTION FOR THE APPEAL

Every year at this time we are reminded that the fate and condition of Israel are our primary Jewish concern, and each year the destiny we have in common with Israel draws us even closer to its people. We have long stopped thinking that there is any distance between us and our brothers and sisters in Israel. History has swept aside the geographic gap between us and how we speak of them and the Jews of the rest of the world in terms of the collective "we" in the first person plural.

During the past year one event in its drama and bold planning and execution provided an historic example of Israel's commitment to freedom. There could be no more pointed lesson for freedom than the fact that the spectacular Israeli rescue of the hostages held in Uganda occurred on the 4th of July – the Bicentennial of the Declaration of American Independence. When we quote the Biblical prophecy that Israel shall be a light unto the nations, it surely can be applied to Entebbe as a message of resistance to terrorism and of positive action to protect human life and freedom addressed by Israel to the rest of the world.

Yet we must not delude ourselves into thinking that Entebbe has solved Israel's problems. As we begin the New Year, we must face up to our responsibility to help our fellow Jews who are tending the eternal flame of Jewish hope and Jewish destiny. We must act with promptness and understanding to strengthen the economy of Israel through our fullest response to the Israel Bond campaign.

2. WHY ISRAEL'S ECONOMY IS IN DIFFICULTY

Ever since the Yom Kippur War, Israel has been waging an economic battle for survival, a battle calling for total mobilization of its people and resources, a battle that could erode the financial stability of the country and stifle its freedom. Because of the unprecedented needs, Israel cannot win if left to its own resources and its own sacrifices. The Israelis are making sacrifices. Taxes are the highest in the world, amounting to about 70 percent. The Government has been forced to cut back on health, education, and other social services. The rate of inflation, which has dropped from a year ago, is still expected to be around 23 percent. Prices of bread, dairy products, and public transportation have been increased sharply during the past year.

Israel is in urgent need of increased income from the sale of Israel Bonds to provide the resources to expand industrial production of exports -- in order to reduce the $4 billion gap in the country's balance of payments, which is chiefly the result of an unprecedented defense budget of more than $3.5 billion.

3. ISRAEL BONDS VITAL TO DEVELOPMENT

Your participation in the Israel Bond effort is needed to furnish the indispensable development funds for production of more exports, for creation of more jobs for new immigrants from Soviet Russia and other countries, and for stepped-up exploration for oil and development of other sources of energy. Israel Bonds have provided more than $3.3 billion for the upbuilding of Israel since 1951. They are needed now more than ever. Israel Bonds must play a vital role in helping to develop science-based and other sophisticated industries which can take advantage of Israel's major natural resource -- the highly skilled and trained men and women in its labor force.

In the year ahead, Israel's trade agreements with the Common Market will present Israel with new opportunities to sell its goods in

Europe. As of next July, Israel manufactured goods will be able to enter the nine member countries of the Common Market duty-free. But such an open door to wider trade will have little meaning for Israel's economy unless Israel has the means to expand its export production immediately. It is an opportunity that must not be missed, for it could revolutionize the country's entire economic future.

4. THE ANSWERS ARE UP TO YOU

On the threshold of the New Year, we must try to find the answers to these questions: Can Israel overcome its financial difficulties? Can Israel develop new sources of energy? Can Israel prevent a rise in unemployment? Can Israel reduce its huge trade deficit by increased production of exports? Can Israel fulfill the potential of the new economic breakthroughs in trade with Europe? The answers to these urgent questions must be expressed in significantly greater participation in the Israel Bond program which is expected to provide a major part of Israel's current Development Budget totaling $1 billion. On this solemn occasion, as we seek guidance for the New Year, we look back not only at the past year but also at the past two hundred years. The links that bind us to America's struggle for independence are as relevant today as the links that bind us to our fellow Jews in Israel and their struggle to rebuild the Jewish homeland in freedom and peace.

5. IN THE SPIRIT OF HAYM SALOMON

In this Bicentennial Year, it is most fitting that we remember a great American and a great Jew -- Haym Solomon -- who devoted his life and his resources in the cause of American independence. While we cannot match the total involvement of this monumental figure, we can follow his example of dedication to the ideals we cherish by supporting the economic independence of the State of Israel. Just as Haym Solomon helped to strengthen the economic foundation of American freedom 200 years ago, we can help to assure Israel's economic future which is so decisive for its progress and welfare.

6. THE DEBT WE OWE

Three years ago world Jewry was in deep mourning for the 3,000 brave young Israelis who fell in the Yom Kippur War. This year we not only recite the Yizkor for them, but also for Lieutenant Colonel Jonathan

Netanyahu, the heroic young officer who was killed in the daring rescue of the hostages in Uganda. We owe a debt to the people of Israel that we can repay only in the coin of concrete action and devoted support. We owe a debt to Colonel Netanyahu and to the men and women who through the years gave their lives for Israel -- and for us, too. Let us respond to the Israel Bond program in that spirit. Let us honor the dead by helping the living create an Israel that shall not know war anymore.

Yom Kippur Sermon
1977

THE TORAH CHARACTERIZES THE Holy Day which we usher in with our services this evening, not as Yom Kippur, the singular form of the word – a Day of Atonement, but as *Yom Kippurim,* in the plural – a Day of Atonements. Why this plural form of the word?

Our answer that readily comes to mind is that if atonement is required to cleanse us from sin, then it must take many multiple atonements to cleanse us from the many sins of which we are individually and collectively guilty every day. Indeed, the confessional prayer, the *Al Het,* which we recite repeatedly throughout the Yom Kippur services, speaks of 44 categories of sin for which we seek atonement. *Yom Kippurim* would, then, indicate that for each sin we require an individual atonement.

But *teshuvah,* repentance, the prime requirement for atonement, is not confined to the High Holy Days. We can, and should, repent every day. Indeed, would it not be better to make atonement daily, as we sin daily? Why then a need for a special day, a *Yom Kippurim* particularly earmarked for atonement? If one can atone on other days, why this day of fasting, sanctification and abstinence from work?

Perhaps Yom Kippur is meant to serve us as a model for everyday living, with its lessons meant as guidelines to influence us throughout the year.

What does the Bible have to say about the observance of the 10th day of Tishrei as the Day of Atonement? In the Book of Numbers, chapter 29, we read as follows, *"Be-asor la-hodesh ha-shevi'i ha-zeh, mikrah kodesh yehiyeh la-khem, ve-anitem et nafshoteikhem; kol melakhah lo ta'asu ve-hikravtem olah l'Adonai* - And ye shall have on the tenth day of this seventh month a convocation of holiness; and ye shall fast; ye shall not do any work therein, but ye shall bring a sacrifice unto the Lord."

Examine the text carefully, and you will note that there are four elements that enter into the observance of Yom Kippur.

First - *mikrah kodesh yehiyeh la-khem* – Ye shall have a convocation of holiness – a gathering, if you will, of the people for the purpose of sanctification. Accordingly, we gather in the synagogue in prayer from nightfall to nightfall on Yom Kippur, to commune with God, and to sanctify His Name. But why only on Yom Kippur? If we take the lesson of Yom Kippur to heart, can we not find the way to imbue everyday with holiness? Life is as sacred as it is fleeting; it must not be wasted, but wisely spent, for it is the one commodity which, when spent, cannot be recovered. "Seven days without prayer makes one weak." Each day must have its holy quality – prayer, Torah, God awareness. These are qualities rarely found in our daily marketplace, far less so in our pursuit of leisure hours.

King Solomon tells us, *"la-kol zeman* - to everything there is a time." Indeed, there is a time for work and a time for relaxing, socializing, and pleasure. But do we make time, as well, for sacredness and seriousness about life and its meaning? If we, in our daily life experience the quality of "the sacred convocation" as we do on Yom Kippur, we can daily earn atonement even without any formal declarations.

Secondly, the Bible tells us, *"ve-anitem et nafshoteikhem* – and Ye shall fast" – and indeed, we do observe the most stringent fast on Yom Kippur, from before sundown to sundown.

What is the significance of fasting? The person who fasts denies himself – for however long or short a time – of a cardinal need of the body. He rejects food to achieve atonement. This lesson of self-denial is crucial, because we American Jews have largely forgotten what self-denial means. Living in an affluent society in which yesterday's luxuries become today's necessities, we are reluctant to do without them, to achieve some worthy objective. How many of us have deprived ourselves of going to the movies, buying unessential luxuries, or skipping a vacation trip, to meet critical charitable needs? Do we forego a trip to Israel so that we can contribute that money to the defense of Israel? The best most of us give are surplus dollars, tax deductions. At worst, we turn our backs to the call of conscience. Nor is money the only criterion. Few of us can demonstrate any self-denial on behalf of our fellow Jews in Russia, in Arab lands, wherever they are threatened. We don't even take an hour off from our activities to join in protest demonstrations, to attend a memorial service for victims of the Holocaust, to participate in community observances of Yom Haatzmaut – Israel Independence Day. But our lack of self-denial applies not only to people distant from us in space and time. It applies to our nearest and dearest. What can be more important to us than our children's upbringing, than their being Jews? And yet it is the exceptional parent – and there are a number in the congregation this evening – who denies himself to give his child an effective Jewish education. Everything precedes it in importance on our tacit scale of priorities. We'll skimp on tuition – can't afford a day school or even an afternoon school – but we can always find the money to buy a car, to remodel the kitchen, to finance a vacation.

We are not even ready to sacrifice a little of our convenience. If adjustments have to be made, let the school make them. We can't forgo the really important things in our life – the Bengals games, the Tacapade rehearsals, the dentist appointments, and most inviolate of all, the dinner hour. We practice no self-denial for our children's Jewish education, and then fail to understand why they don't take Hebrew school seriously. We permit them – nay encourage them to drop out of Jewish school after Bar Mitzva – and can't understand why our children in college reject the Jewish heritage. We don't fast for Jewish learning? Why should they? Self-denial as exemplified by our fast day means that we should have no rest when our brothers in Israel live on the brink of annihilation, that we have no right to sleep peacefully in bed, when millions throughout the world can find no place to rest their heads, no food to still their hunger. This then, is the implication of this second element of Yom Kippur for our daily life.

Thirdly, Yom Kippur proclaims, *"kol melakhah lo ta'asu* - Ye shall not do any work." Our complete withdrawal from work underscores our conception of the importance of enhancing life with a human dimension. We are not machines nor are we beasts of burden. There are values of life, of the mind, of the heart, and of the spirit, that are significant, that need to be cultivated and nurtured. We must periodically desist from work that we may find the time to share with our families, with our fellow men, with our God.

If today is *Shabbat Shabbaton*, the Sabbath of Sabbaths, we are reminded that there is a Sabbath every week to draw us away from the mundane world of work, there is a shul to pull us out of the "rat race" of the market, there is a Torah to enrich our spirit as work enriches our bank account, and the companionships of our family and our friends to give meaning to our existence.

And finally, the fourth element of Yom Kippur is, *"ve-hikravtem olah l'Adonai* - ye shall bring a sacrifice unto the Lord." Why did we bring an offering in Temple days? Does God need the flesh of the animal that is sacrificed on the altar? The prophet Isaiah tells us, *"Lamah li rov zivheikhem yomar Adonai savati olot eilim ve-helev me-ri'im* - To what purpose is the multitude of your sacrifices unto me, saith the Lord. I am full of the burnt offerings of rams and the fat of fed beasts ... Put away the evil of your doings from before Mine eyes, cease to do evil. Learn to do well; seek justice, relieve the oppressed, judge the fatherless, and plead for the widow." It is not the flesh of the sacrifice that God craves, but the spirit of sacrifice which impels man to shed his complacency and to learn compassion, to shun evil and embrace virtue, to remain not aloof to the needs of the unfortunate – next door or across the seas, but to give of himself to alleviate the sufferings and still the pangs of hunger. It is the sacrifice that is the condition, according to Isaiah for the atonement. *"Im yi'heyu hatoteikhem ka-shanim ka-sheleg yalbinu, im yadimu ha-tolah ka tzemer yi'heyu."* Live the life of sacrifice, promises the prophet and, "though your sins be as scarlet they shall be white as snow, though they be red as crimson, they shall be as wool."

These four elements: *mikrah kodesh* (a holy convocation), *ve-anitem et nafshoteikhem* (ye shall fast), *kol melakhah lo ta'asu* (ye shall not do any work), and *ve-hikravtem olah* (ye shall bring a sacrifice) are what make Yom Kippur a Day of Atonement; practiced every day, they can make every day a *Yom Kippurim*, a Day of Atonements. This is the challenge of the plural form of the name of this holy day to us.

In the spirit of *Yom Kippurim* we pray for the speedy fulfillment of the prophetic reassurance, *"Ki ba-yom ha-zeh ye'khapeir aleikhem le-taheir Etkhem mikol hatoteikhem* - On this Day Atonement shall be made for us, cleansing us from all our sins before God" this day and every day, and ushering in for us all Israel and all mankind a year of peace and surety, of life and health, material success and spiritual fulfillment, a year in which the four elements of Yom Kippur will daily find and echo in our hearts and in our deeds, and let us say, Amen.

Influenced by the Writings of Rabbi Simon Dolgin

Yom Kippur Sermon
1979
A Holy People – A Dread Of Sin

TODAY I WANT TO talk to you about two short phrases from our Yom Kippur service. They are not major passages. The ark is not left opened for them and we do not rise in our seats to recite them. The cantor does not caress them with this voice, but more often than not passes quickly over them, saving his voice for the better-known and more conspicuous portions of the service. And yet I would venture to suggest that these two short phrases encompass and conceal two basic concepts essential to our survival as a people. In a sense, all the rest of the service is mere commentary and explication of these brief words.

They are recited by the hazzan and the congregation in the Shaharit service right after the Barkhu, the traditional call to prayer. The first phrase is, *"Slah le-goy kadosh, be-yom kadosh, marom ve-kadosh -* Forgive this holy people on this holy day, Thou Who art exalted and holy." At first glance the phrase seems simple and innocuous enough. And yet, on reflection, it begs explication. That God is holy and this day of Yom Kippur is holy seems self-evident. But what makes us, the Jewish people, a *goy kadosh,* a holy people? Surely many of us act throughout the year in ways that may be far removed from what is ordinarily considered and thought of as "holy." Are we then holy on this *yom kadosh,* this Holy Day when we stand in prayer and penitence before God who is *marom ve-kadosh,* holy and exalted? Or does the holiness of which the prayer speaks extend to the other 364 days of the year as well?

To attempt an answer to this question, one must look more closely at the word *kadosh*. With its many permutations, *kadosh* is probably one of the better-known words in our Jewish vocabulary. We chant the *kiddush,* recite the *kaddish,* we rise for the *kedushah,* we entrust the *hevreh kadishah* with funeral arrangements, we mourn on Tisha B'av the destruction of the Beit Hamikdash, we recite the formula *"asher kideshanu be-mitzvotav"* every time we make a *brakhah,* we scold our children for the mess, the *hekdesh* which they make ... the list goes on and on. When a farmer in ancient Israel wished to present an animal to the Temple as a sacrifice, that animal became *kodesh.* In ancient pagan cults that go back to Biblical times, fertility rites were practiced in the heathen temples by temple prostitutes. Such a woman was referred to as a *kadeishah* in the Bible. When a couple is married under the *huppah,* the ceremony is known as *kiddushin.* What is the common denominator, the common thread, the root meaning of *kadosh* from which all these terms – some holy, some decidedly profane – derive? The answer is that the root meaning of *kadosh* is not, as commonly translated, "holy" but rather "set apart." Follow this meaning and all the derivations become clear. The *kiddush* is the prayer in which we declare the Sabbath is a day set apart from the rest of the week. The *kiddush* not only sets apart and separates the various sections of the service, but it, and the *kaddish* as well, declare the transcendence of God. The farmer set apart his cow from the rest of the herd to be sacrificed in the house devoted and set apart for worship. The temple courtesan was set apart from other women by her vocation. The bride, in the ceremony of the wedding, is consecrated and set apart exclusively for her husband, and so the list goes on and on.

Let us go back to the original question. What does the *mahzor* mean when it characterizes the Jewish people as a *goy kadosh,* a holy people, and the meaning becomes clear. We are a people set apart, or, a parallel phrase in the Amidah recited on Shabbos afternoon would have it, a *"goy ehad ba-aretz* - a people that is unique on all the earth." We have an identity and an individuality that shapes us and molds us and that, whether we wish to acknowledge it or attempt to deny it, sets us apart from the nations of the world.

This uniqueness of the Jewish people has been attested to, over and over again, whether to laud us or damn us, from the dawn of our history to our own times. The Torah tells us of an incident that took place when our ancestors wandered through the desert on the way to the Promised Land. As they passed the land of Moab, Balak, the Moabite king, called on the heathen prophet Bilaam to "curse this people that has come out of Egypt." Bilaam hastened to do the king's bidding but was prevented from doing so by God. Instead, as he lifted his eyes and saw the peaceful encampment of the Israelites, he burst into words of praise, *"Ki mei-rosh tzurim er'enu, u-mi-gevaot ashurenu* - For I see it from the summit of the rocks and from the hills do I gaze on it." *"Hen am le-vad yishkon, u-va-goyim lo yit'hashov* - It is a people that shall dwell apart and not reckon itself among the nations."

The recognition that we are a *goy kadosh,* a holy people, a people set apart from all others, has followed us from Bilaam's day to our own. It has served as the pretext for oppressors and tyrants from Haman to Hitler who sought to destroy us. It has served as a source of strength and as the rallying cry of the heroes and patriots of our people who sought to preserve us. Where we clung to our identity, to our uniqueness, we persevered and flourished. Where we sought to escape it, to deny it, it was thrust upon us by our enemies as a pretext to destroy us. Our long history is replete with examples of both affirmation and denial. The ten northern tribes of Israel renounced their Jewish distinctiveness. Within several generations after their conquest by the Assyrians they had ceased to exist. The two southern tribes clung to their uniqueness. Even Babylonian exile could not extinguish their flame.

The city of Alexandria in ancient times had a strong and powerful Jewish community. They were a flourishing people, great writers, learned scholars, mighty warriors, and wealthy merchants and artisans. With the spread of Hellenism, however, Alexandrian Jewry turned its back on its Hebrew heritage and uniqueness. They assumed Greek names; practiced Greek customs; neglected the Hebrew language, the Hebrew Bible and the Hebrew prayers, and substituted the Greek vernacular of their neighbors. They discarded their Jewish ways and aped the ways of the pagan world. It was not long before their neighbors, the very same one whose lifestyle they copied so assiduously, turned on them, and the great Alexandrian Jewish community came to an end. On the opposite side of the spectrum is the experience of Ezra and Nehemia. The handful of Jews who had returned from Babylon to rebuild the Temple in Jerusalem had fallen upon evil ways. They had gradually come to assume the ways of their heathen neighbors, to intermarry with them, to worship their gods. Ezra and Nehemia succeeded in persuading them to reaffirm their status as a *goy kadosh*. They renounced their pagan ways, divested themselves of their pagan wives, to God with all their heart, accepted the Torah as their constitution, and entrusted themselves to God's Providence. Because their desire to be a *goy kadosh* burned so brightly in their hearts they succeeded against all odds. From this humble beginning developed the strong and powerful Second Commonwealth of Israel.

What makes us a *goy kadosh?* First -- our heritage. Whether or not we wish to acknowledge it, we are the Chosen People, selected by God not for honors and glory, but to be dedicated to His service and to be a light unto the nations. When the children of Israel encamped at the foot of Mount Sinai preparing to receive the Torah, God spoke to them from the mountain, *"Ve-atah im shamoa tishme'u be-koli u-shmartem et briti –* And now if you listen to My Voice and will keep My covenant – *Vi-heyitem li segulah mikol ha-amim, ki li kol ha-aretz -* Then you shall be Mine own treasure from among all peoples; for all the world is Mine – *Atem ti'hiyu li mamlekhet kohanim, ve-goy kadosh -* And you shall be unto Me a kingdom of priests and a holy people."

But if we are to truly be a *goy kadosh,* then merely the accident of being born into this Chosen People is not enough. It is not enough to have uniqueness thrust upon us. Among the pitiful of Hitler's victims were the assimilated German Jews who went to their death not comprehending how this could be happening to them, to loyal and super-patriotic Germans who happened to be *Deutsche des Moseishen Glaubens,* Germans of the Mosaic persuasion, Jews by birth, it's true, but first and foremost loving sons of the *Vaterland.*

A *goy kadosh* is not only a matter of our Biblical heritage; it is a matter, as well, of our conscious affirmation of our individuality and uniqueness. It requires us not only to be passively aware of our heritage, but to actively and proudly affirm it by our actions and our resolves. How do we act Jewishly? By supporting Jewish causes, by becoming Jewishly knowledgeable, by participating in the life of the Jewish community, by sharing in the struggles of our brethren in Israel, Russia, and throughout the world, by practicing the precepts of our religion. If we wish to be a *goy kadosh* we must be aware that from the very beginning of our peoplehood, from Sinai on, we were told clearly and unequivocally that Divine Providence is not ours for the asking as a Chosen People, but is conditional on, *"Im shamoa tishme'u be-koli,"* our doing God's will. And so, on this Day of Atonement, with repentance in our hearts, we turn to God with the prayer, *"Selah le-goy kadosh, be-yom kadosh, marom ve-kadosh* - Forgive this holy people on this holy day, Thou Who art exalted and holy." This brings us to the second verse in our prayer book on which I want to comment. Following the verse we have just discussed, the hazzan chants, *"Hatanu Tzureinu slah lanu yotzreinu –* We have sinned, O God; Forgive us, Our Creator." This request in various forms recurs with great frequency in the Yom Kippur service. What is its significance? I'd like to suggest to you that its importance lies not merely in our repeating the whole catalogue of sins of which we are cumulatively guilty, not merely in our proclaiming that all of us are responsible for the sins of each of us, but in the very fact that we acknowledge the concept of sin as real and present in our lives. When we acknowledge sin, we affirm as well that there exists a body of absolute moral values and religious laws, the violation of which is a breach of God's will, a sin. Sin, or better, the awareness of sin, was a real factor in the everyday life of our parents' and grandparents' generation. They knew that one must not only do *mitzvot,* but also refrain from doing *aveirot* that is a synonym for *het,* sin, was very much a part of their everyday vocabulary. It was an *aveirah* to transgress the Shabbos, an *aveirah* to eat non-kosher food, an *aveirah* to marry outside of the faith. It was even, if you recall, an *aveirah "arois tzu warfen" –* to throw out something that still had some useful life in it.

On the Shabbos proceeding Rosh Hodesh we customarily ask for God's blessings in the coming month. Among the blessings for which we pray is, *"hayim she-yesh ba-hem yirat shamayim ve-yirat het –* a life of piety and dread of sin." Dread of sin is a blessing. We pray, not for absolution form the consequence of sin, not for dread of punishment for the sins we have committed, but for a life which is imbued with a consciousness and awareness of sin, not as an abstraction but as a very real and concrete force in life to which we must not succumb. *"Hatanu Tzureinu slah lanu yotzreinu –* We have sinned, O God; Forgive us, Our Creator.

Today, our consciousness of sin is at very low ebb. Were it not for the annual visit to the synagogue or the occasional exhortation of fundamentalist Christian preachers on TV, who knows if we'd come across the word at all. It's certainly not part of our vocabulary as it once was part of our grandparents' vocabulary. Psychiatrists, psychologists, and sociologists have coined new phrases that have displaced the concept of sin in our minds. Today we suffer from anxieties, complexes and neuroses, we are subject to compulsions and psychoses, we reach to deep-seated repression and depression, we act out of cultural conditioning and respond to culture shock, we even have been allowed the luxury of guilt in big doses – but you'll look in vain for the concept of sin. And along with the disappearance of the concept of *yirat het,* of dread of sin, has come the dismantling of our framework of absolute moral and religious standards ordained by God in favor of glib and convenient theories of relativism that are peddled as science and as fact. Morality, we are told, is not absolute and permanent. No, it is nothing more than a matter of social mores that differ from culture to culture and from age to age. Not the word of God, but the cultural norms of the community dictate our standards of behavior. Morality is relative and changeable, and everyone should be doing "his own thing." Small wonder, then, that our media, in particular our TV, glamorize and present as acceptable and normative the abominations and perversions of our moral ethic. Turn to any soap opera, to any situation comedy, to any talk show, to any dramatic series, and what do you see? Honesty, fidelity, chastity, virginity, and virtue, are not part of the daily life portrayed on the electronic tube. Such behavior, if it is acknowledged to exist at all, is portrayed rather quizzically as "real square," dated and absurd, at times smiled at tolerantly and patronizingly, but more often than not treated as laughable and ludicrous, terribly anachronistic and out of step with modern times. No, the real world, as we see it represented on TV, is a world in which the virtues of the past are relegated to the attic, a world of violence, cunning and deceit, a world peopled with con-men, prostitutes, and high-powered unprincipled businessmen, a world in which "alternative life styles" – homosexuality, live-in friends, marital infidelity, flagrant sex, and regular use of alcohol and drugs – are the socially accepted and perfectly acceptable and legitimate norms of behavior. Bombarded by this daily onslaught of hedonism, permissiveness and self-indulgence, of promiscuity and self gratification rooted in the bedrock of relativism, of everything goes, of each man his own determiner of what's right for him, no wonder we, and particularly the younger generation which was not brought up with the concept of *mitzvah* and *aveirah,* are in dire danger not only of sinning, but of forgetting the very concept of sin and of the moral code which is its obverse. *Hatanu Tzureinu.*

We have sinned, O God, by losing sight of our *yirat het,* our sense of sin, our dread of sin.

The twin concepts of *goy kadosh,* our self-perception as a unique people set apart, and of *yirat het,* of the dread of sin, were two of the most potent and dynamic forces in Jewish survival through the ages. If we wish to survive in the future we must recapture these twin concepts, for ourselves and for our children. We must cultivate an appreciation of our Jewish uniqueness, of our standing apart from the faceless masses because we are a *goy kadosh,* a proud and restless people which has given the world way out of proportion to its size in humanity and compassion, in religion and morality, in science and industry, in culture and refinement – and, moreover, a people that has much to give in the future as it has in the past, because we are an *"Am Segulah* - God's Chosen People" who will not rest, who cannot rest, until "the world is perfected under the kingdom of the Almighty."

And we must recapture and cultivate our ancestors' understanding that there is a moral order in the universe that is unchangeable and immutable because it is the will of God, and that to defy this moral constant is not neurosis, not compulsion, but sin pure and simple. Truly we must strive to lead our lives in consonance with *yirat shamayim ve-yirat het,* with true piety and with dread of sin, if we are to emerge from the morass of relativistic immorality in which we wallow today.

This, then, is the message of Yom Kippur. This is the insight that we must bring to bear on our prayer books as we ask for atonement from God. Earnestly and humbly we pray, *"Slah le goy kadosh, be-yom kadosh, marom ve-kadosh* - Forgive this holy people on this holy day, Thou Who art exalted and holy. *Hatanu Tzureinu slah lanu yotzreinu* - We have sinned, O God; Forgive us, Our Creator." Amen.

Yom Kippur Sermon
1980
Prayer For All Ages

ONCE A DISCIPLE ASKED his rabbi, "Tell me, rabbi, what do you do before you pray?" Whereupon the rabbi replied, "I pray that when I pray it should be with all my heart."

We meet tonight in the synagogue on the eve of the most sacred day of our year, about to recite the first in a series of prayers that will take us the better part of the day to complete, praying that our prayers truly come from the heart, praying that our prayers ascend to the seat of judgment, praying that our prayers be answered.

It is only appropriate, therefore, to pause for a few moments to reflect on what prayer is and what it ought to be.

There are some people who think of prayer only as something we have to do at times of anguish and extremity -- when a beloved is sick when great sorrow has befallen us, when we have come to a great tragedy or are confronted by an enormous danger. It is then that even those of us who do not habitually pray find ourselves impelled to join in prayer. When the sailors upon the ship in which Jonah was fleeing from his vision saw the storm arising, they fell to their knees in prayer. Abraham Lincoln wrote in the darkest moments of the Civil War, "I was driven to my knees by the overwhelming conviction that there was no other place to go." When all about us there is darkness, when in our hearts there is fear and apprehension and anxiety -- whatever our theological beliefs may be, we are impelled to pray. A modern psychologist has said that prayer is normal; men pray because they cannot help themselves. Prayer is part of the need of the human being, and there are circumstances in every life when we resort to prayer.

Sometimes people think that prayers are what we teach our children. How frequently parents have boasted that their children know the prayers to be said upon arising and the prayer to be said before retiring as night. We think of children as requiring the training of prayer. We are not sure whether they will follow this training, but we feel it obligatory upon us as parents to at least subject them to this training. There are more sophisticated people who say that prayer belongs to the early history of mankind, to its childhood. Children are poetic; children are half witches with fantasy. It is appropriate, therefore, that the poetry that was created in the early youth of the human race should be given over to children.

Sometimes we think of prayer as something for the old, those who have already passed the active years of their lives, who have already entered upon that twilight zone where there is only one eventuality ahead. Then one feels like prayer. Once I passed a beautiful temple in New York, and outside there was a sign: "Please come in for meditation and prayer." I was not interested in meditation or prayer at that time; I was interested in the architecture of that house of prayer, and so I went in. On this weekday afternoon, there was a small group of people sitting in the quiet and somewhat subdued atmosphere of the temple, engaged in prayer. As I looked at the group, I did not see one young person there. It was the elderly men and women who had come to pray. And so generally we associate prayer with old people. Their creative life is passed. There are no challenging problems, no new frontiers, so these sunset days they may as well spend in prayer.

If this will be our attitude, prayer will be reserved only for emergency hours, for children, and for the aged. We shall be missing all the possibilities of prayer, and all the opportunities of these High Holy Days.

Prayer is not an easy way of getting God to do what He ought to do, and neither is it a way of getting Him to do what we ought to do. There is no escape from the duty that lies upon us. Prayer will not offer us a refuge from the problems that trouble us. Prayer does, however, offer us the opportunity to raise ourselves and our lives to a higher peak. Prayer, if performed in that spirit, will put us in a better position, far better equipped to deal with the harassments and the dilemmas of our lives.

Prayer takes us into a large universe. It pushes out the walls of normal existence. How small is the area in which most of us live! During our vacations, we may take trips abroad and see distant lands, but most of the time the majority of us lead lives that are local and parochial. All of us live in restricted areas of our own concerns -- of our families, of our own offices and needs, of our own resentments, hates, and prejudices. How important it is that now and then we go out into the great open space of the universe and let the vast breeze that come from distant places blow in upon our confined lives. How important it is to capture for a moment the large perspective that lets us see ourselves as part of a larger universe.

Prayer is the opportunity to rise to our highest level. Sometimes we are told that we cannot do much with human nature. The realists think they have attained the ultimate wisdom when they say we cannot change human nature. Without entering into any philosophical analysis of the subject, suffice it to say that in human nature there are wide ranges that in a very real sense a human being can move from one extreme to another, can rise from the depths to the heights. The vicious criminal reflects human nature, but so do the saint, the prophet, and the psalmist, the scientist and the artist. They, too, are expressions of human nature. On which rung shall we stand? At which end of the spectrum shall we live? This is determined by us.

We live generally in a competitive world. Competition arouses our combativeness, our pugnacity. It pits us against our neighbor. It becomes a contest, an Olympic game. You have seen pictures of athletes who did not come in first. The camera has caught the grief and disappointment that are engraved upon their faces. There must also be resentment in their hearts against those who came in first. Within all of us, however, there is also unexpressed and unevoked kindliness. I have seen people in emergencies display so much tenderness that I said to myself, "It must have been there all the time; it required an extraordinary situation to elicit it." Prayer offers an outlet to that in us which is fine and delicate, to that which is not competitive, but embraces all men in the mantle of concern and solicitude. Prayer seeks to release the good imprisoned within us.

In this spirit, then, let us approach the opportunity for prayer not as a burden, not as a tradition, not as a habit into which we have fallen, but as a great privilege, as a means of opening new doors, as conferring upon us the possibility of enriching our own lives and of attaining the highest stature we have ever attained before. When we approach prayer in this spirit, our prayers will undoubtedly be answered.

EULOGY

The American Israelite
Cincinnati, Ohio
May 26, 2011

THE ISRAELITE IS SADDENED to learn of the death on May 13, 2011 (9 Iyar, 5771) of Max Frankel. Although some will remember with fondness how Frankel led the auxiliary services for the High Holidays for many years at Golf Manor Synagogue, and his extraordinary Jewish Culture & Arts program which featured noted artists and performers several times each year, Frankel is perhaps best remembered in local circles for his 25 years of dedicated service as the Executive Director of the Bureau of Jewish Education. At the time of his retirement 14 years ago, Frankel was the most senior in length of service of all directors of Bureaus and Central Agencies for Jewish Education in the United States. His administration of the BJE was marked by tireless effort and numerous innovations that made the now defunct Federation-funded agency an effective and respected partner of all area Jewish schools. Many of the programs and services the BJE provided year-round, were introduced, developed or expanded during Frankel's tenure. Among the better-known of these were: the Jewish Teacher Center; the Jewish Media Center; the TIKVAH Juniors and Seniors programs for the develop-mentally disabled; the Florence Melton Adult Mini-School; the Jewish Heritage Seminars for public school teachers; Professional Enrichment and Growth Subsidies and Incentive Grant Programs for teachers in Cincinnati's religious schools; Teen programs e.g. the March of the Living trip to Poland and Israel, the Panim el Panim Youth Mission to Washington, and the Teacher Assistant Program, training day school Junior high school students for service in Cincinnati's congregational schools; the year-round Discount Jewish Book Store; and the much beloved Jewish Book Fair and Entertainment Series ... the list could go on.

As a Yiddish speaking twelve-year-old, Frankel immigrated with his parents to the United States in 1940 after experiencing two years of forced house arrest in Vienna, Austria during WWII. Only narrowly escaping with his parents on the last passenger ship out of the port of Trieste, Italy, Frankel's four older siblings were sent ahead of them to America, England and Holland to escape the escalating Nazi terror. Despite the fact that each survived the war (his older brother Hesh had harrowing stories of his near death experiences in several concentration camps), Frankel's oldest brother, Efraim, sadly died only shortly after arriving in America.

After arriving in America, and graduating from the Yeshiva Israel Salanter (now SAR Academy in Riverdale, NY), Frankel went on to attend Yeshiva University's high school and college. A cum laude graduate of the Teachers Institute of Yeshiva University and of Yeshiva College of Liberal Arts, Frankel went on to serve in several prominent educational settings in Rochester, Erie, Boston, Philadelphia, and finally, Cincinnati. All told, Frankel served 48 years as a master educator and educational administrator. Messages of condolence can be sent to the Frankel family at davidtfrankel@gmail.com. Described at his funeral as a gentle, kind-hearted, and affable man who loved a good joke and always had a book in his hand and a song in his heart, Frankel was laid to rest by his loving family at the Beth David Cemetery in Elmont, NY (the same cemetery as his oldest brother Efraim) and is survived by his wife of 58 years, Gloria Frankel of Cincinnati OH; their four sons, Edwin (Anna) Frankel of Columbus, OH; Jeffrey Frankel of Commack, NY; Daniel (Jodi) Frankel of Suwanee, GA; and David (Cindy) Frankel of Kew Gardens Hills, NY; his older brother Hesh (Miriam) Frankel of Givatayim, Israel; his oldest sibling Molly Frankel Neuman of Englewood, NJ; and his ten loving grandchildren, Joshua, Elisheva, Sara, Dustin, Kaitlyn, Sydney, Sarah, Shayna Laya, Shira, and Miriam. Shiva was held at David's home in Kew Gardens Hills, NY through Friday, May 20.

EULOGY

Edwin Ronald "Efraim Reuven ben Meir" Frankel
b. October 17, 1953

As I've gathered my thoughts over the past two days since I first learned that my Dad passed, part of me says y'know you're in mourning and you should be sad and upset. On the other hand, here's a man who's been in pain for the last several months of his life who is in a better place now and whose every act from the time I was born was one of *zekhut* to all *B'nai Adam*. If anybody ever lived up to the ideal of, *"mikabel kol adam be-seiver panim yafot - receive everyone with a cheerful face,"* it was Dad. If it could be said of anyone that he was *"ke-tocho ke-boro – his essence was as his appearance,"* he talked the talk and walked the walk, it was Dad.

Three weeks ago, in what would be our last Torah conversation, I was telling my Father that I was invited to write a *peirush* for a new *siddur* that's going to be coming out, God knows when. And every person who contributed to it was asked to comment on a *tefillah* that meant the most to them. And I told him which one I was going to write on and he was interested. So I asked him if he was going to write on a particular *tefillah* which would he write on? And he quoted a *kapitil Tehillim* that we daven every *Shabbos* morning, *"Le-David be-shanoto et tamo lifnei Avimelekh va-yegarsheihu va-yeilakh."* He said this was his favorite of the *mizmorim* and especially the part with the *pasuk*, *"Mi ha-ish he-hafetz hayim, oheiv yamim lirot tov. Netzor le-shonkha me-rah, u-sefatekha mi-dabeir mirmah. Tzur me-rah va-asei tov, bakeish shalom ve-radfeihu. – Who's the person who desires life, who loves days and seeing good in them? Stop your tongue from speaking evil, your lips from guile. Cast yourself away from evil and do good. Seek peace and chase it."*

If anything capitalized or summarized my Father's life as an educator, as a Father, as my Mother's husband and best friend for 58 years, it's that *pasuk*.

EULOGY
Jeffrey Alan "Yitzhak ben Meir" Frankel
b. October 19, 1955

EVERYTHING I AM IS a part of Dad. So many memories and I
remember them all. Although I was born in 1955 in Rochester, New York,
I can vividly remember when Dad moved us to Erie, Pennsylvania so he
could start a promising new career as the Executive Director of the Erie
Jewish Center. Our family was smaller then. It was only Edwin, Mom,
Dad, and me. I still remember the drive from Rochester to Erie in our blue
car. Good times. Year later, I remember when Dad had an outpatient
procedure to remove a cyst on his backside. I had one too. Back then the
doctors used wire to stich Dad up. Oh, how I remember the scream Dad let
out when he mistakenly used alcohol to clean his wound. Oy, poor Dad!
He tried to put out the sting by sitting in a pool of water. It didn't help
much.

When we moved from Erie to Philadelphia, I can remember being
driven by Dad to nursery school. Dad was the Executive Director of the
school at the Oxford Circle Jewish Community Center. I spent a few years
attending school at OCJCC. I knew the place so well that people would
come to me instead of Dad with questions on where they could find this or
that. Dad and Mom took a lot of pride in that. I even remember Dad
introducing me to my nursery school teacher and her family.

Perhaps one of our family's most infamous tales is related to a game
of Cowboys and Indians that Edwin and I played as kids. Edwin tells a
different version of the story, but we both remember that I threw a fork at
Edwin that became lodged in his head. Boy oh boy, was Mom scared. She
frantically called Dad at work. She was frightened and anxious. His

response was simple and to the point, "Pull it out." That's kind of how Dad was in most instances. He didn't sugar coat things. He was compassionate, but he told it to you straight, simple, and to the point.

So many memories. I remember how excited Mom and Dad were when Mom was pregnant in Philadelphia with Danny and four years later with David. When I was a kid I can remember that Mom and Dad were smokers. Back then, we didn't know how dangerous smoking was. By the time Danny was born, Dad had given up smoking. If you'd ask him about it, he didn't claim to have given it up; he was simply going without. The truth is that he went cold turkey. He just decided one day, and that was that. Dad was like that too. Once he made his mind up there was no looking back.

Dad always looked out for me and my memories of him are too numerous to put into words.

Everything I am is a part of Dad.

EULOGY

Daniel Bennett "Daniel Barukh ben Meir" Frankel
b. December 26, 1963

IT HAS BEEN NEARLY a year since Dad's passing and, to me, it still doesn't feel like he is gone. While Dad's absence is obvious, for me ... it still feels like he is home in Cincinnati ... even though I know sadly, this isn't the case. It is said that the deceased live on through our memories. This couldn't be truer. I can picture Dad telling one of his jokes, singing *zemiros, davening* in the morning, and leading Musaf ... in fact, I can almost hear him. Unfortunately, the actual words are too muffled ... the melodies too quiet. I can, however, just about make out his voice or the way he would say my name.

Dad wasn't a very athletic man. I understand he played handball, till his hands turned bright red, as a young man. I don't really remember Dad playing many ball games with me, though I suspect we may have played toss at one time. I remember playing "pig" or "horse" basketball with him once or twice. I also remember him playing ping-pong. I was amused as a kid that he could not ride a bike but I could. How could anyone not know how to ride a bike? He didn't really swim; rather, he would do a terrific dead man's float. We did go swimming a few times including at the Atlantic Ocean (at the Chasen's house on Avon Beach), at the JCC, Houston Woods, and on our big summer trip to/from Florida. I think my first actual swim lesson was at Avon Beach. Dad had me on his shoulders as he walked out into the ocean. A wave came and knocked me off. I'd like to say I swam back to shore on my own. In reality, the wave must have carried me most of the way as the next thing I remember is coughing, sputtering, gagging, and crying in the shallow water on the beach. Oops.

I remember Dad visiting Yavneh and how the kids were all a bit intimidated by him. They had no reason to feel that way and learned quickly that he was a nice man ... and just a man. I can remember him administering the *Hidon Ha-Tanakh,* though I think I only took it once. I did participate in an art contest once that Dad was judging. I did a miniature version of Jerusalem or the Temple Mount in sugar cubes. I won a first prize blue ribbon in that competition. Dad was a judge and I caught a lot of grief over nepotism for that. He claimed I won fair and square. I still believe him ... the man never lied.

Dad did not try to impose his beliefs on others. I don't know if it was his motto but I can remember the words "live and let live" being a recurring theme in our house. I don't remember Dad getting upset with people very often. Generally, he wouldn't say very much if he disagreed. That isn't to say he wouldn't stand up for himself ... or his family. Rather, he was careful whether to engage. Most of the time, he would listen, say his goodbyes, and then walk away from discussions that had turned into debates, knowing that he was right, as it just wasn't worth an argument. I think it was more annoying to us that he didn't rub at least some people's noses in it. Dad would say the people that knew better knew that he was right.

While I can't interact with Dad physically any longer, I still have a sense of him being near. I can still imagine or remember him:

- sitting in the family room watching baseball on TV (or whatever program Mom had programmed to pop up) or doing a puzzle while eating a piece of fruit or some peanuts,

- sitting at the head of the table in the kitchen (on Shabbos or weekday dinner) or at the head of the dining room table for *Yuntif* dinner (specifically during our family *seders*),

- at *Shul* (whether Roselawn *Shul,* Ohav Shalom, KI, Golf Manor, the *Shtiebel,* and even *B'nai Tzedek)* singing with the hazzan loudly enough that you could hear his voice above everyone else's,

- In his office at the Bureau either behind his desk looking very important or running around the office doing this or that (cataloging library books, collating/folding/ stuffing envelopes), up a ladder finding places for books behind books on the high shelves of the office book store,

- Talking about the upcoming book fair, artist exhibits, and culture and arts programs,

- Singing on our walks and drives

- Building his *sukkah* and how proud he was to share the experience with us and then to show off what we built to others,

- Correcting me during my Bar Mitzvah lessons and our epic battles,

- Teaching me how to wear my *tefillin,*

- Asking how I am doing,

- And more.

In fact, I can still hear the resonance of his voice:

- while *davening* at home and in *shul* (in front of the *Amud*),

- singing *zemiros* Friday night, Saturday afternoon, and Saturday evening,

- Teaching me to *daven* and *lein,*

- singing his songs (Mairzy Doats, Shoo Fly Pie, Let's Go Fly A Kite, Peanut Pat'em on the Popo, 76 Trombones (Lead the Big Parade), Oh You Can't Get To Heaven, He's Got the Whole World In His Hands (Mom and David reminded me of this one), *David Melekh Yisrael, Ve-David Yefei Einayim, Sisu et Yerushalayim,* and more,

- and when speaking on the phone or talking in person.

These images and sounds (and more) are trapped in my brain. They are whispers now … almost annoying to have but that I am unwilling to forget. I wish I could record these experiences so that I could play them back and share these memories with others, however the technology for this does not exist as of yet.

Dad taught a strong work ethic, how to be a Jew, how to *daven,* and how to treat everyone as you'd like them to treat you. At times, I feel like the song "Cats in the Cradle" describe our father ... and me. Who was Max Frankel? He was the Director of the Bureau of Jewish Education, he was our mother's husband, and he was our dad. He took care of his family. He worked hard almost every day and rarely got sick. If he did ... I don't think we'd really know it. He woke up every morning and lay in bed for a while ... I supposed planning his day. He then washed and shaved, dressed, then *davened.* He rarely left the house before his "morning ritual." One of the times I remember him leaving the house before completing his "ritual" was to look for Shelly, our first dog. She wasn't really our dog yet. She had followed me home from a party and was spending the night in our garage. She ran off during the night after she was let out to go to the bathroom. The next morning, he was out looking for her before cleaning up and before *davening.* Dad was a gentle man, a soft-spoken man, and a realist. He saw everything very clearly. Dad was a caring and kind man. I don't think Dad had a dishonest bone in his body. He lived what he preached. He was trustworthy. I remember the battles he had with Mom about him needing to come home by a certain time for dinner. I'm sorry Jodi, I am very much the same as him in that regard. I don't remember him yelling or ever being very angry at me. I remember him giving me a few deserved spankings ... and several lectures for my misbehavior. I don't remember him saying, "I told you so."

The day Dad died I was at work. It will be a day I never forget. Mom called to tell me what had happened. Intellectually, I understood what she said but I just couldn't believe it. I was in shock but continued working. I had to finish ... as much for them as for me. I needed to work or I would have really lost it as there was not much to do while preparations for Dad's funeral were being put into motion. That Shabbos in *shul* was one of the hardest. I am normally a leader in the *shul* when it comes to singing the *davening.* That day, I could barely utter a peep. I could not fathom my Father's passing. The realization that he would never stand next to me in *shul* again, that my being at home in the synagogue, and my *neshamah* were as a result of what he sacrificed for me, were all-overwhelming. My Jewish education, ability to read Hebrew, chant prayers, lead services, *lein* Torah and Haftarah ... were all his doing and now he was gone.

To conclude, sitting around our dining room table growing up wouldn't have felt normal without Dad's humor, double-entendres, limericks, sex talks, and yes, poop discussions. Dad allowed these, though the word *"Nu"* did leave his lips when we went too far or carried on for too long. He was not a prude but though there were limits, nothing was "off limits." We all knew where the liquor cabinet was and it was never locked. We were trusted and we were loved. We were given an amazing childhood, whether we could see it at the time or not. Finally, we would joke that the only sure things in life were death and taxes. Death wasn't feared or unexpected. Rather, we just didn't expect it on May 13, 2011 ... I didn't expect it. I miss my Father.

I love you Dad.

EULOGY

David Tovya "David Tovya ben Meir" Frankel
b. September 19, 1967

WHAT CAN I SAY? My Father was an extraordinary man. Kind. Gentle. Extremely funny. He loved a good joke and knew how to tell one. I can't do that. My Father was also a man of tremendous integrity and honesty. He was an extremely educated man, but he was at the same time absolutely unpretentious. He was affable and easy to befriend. Growing up in his home it's hard for me to remember a morning when he wasn't singing, as he got dressed. He just always had a song in his heart. My Father was a voracious reader, as is my Mother. He particularly loved a good jigsaw puzzle or word game. He especially loved starting with a 10 or more letter word and seeing how many smaller words he could find within it. We gave up on playing Scrabble with him when I was a little boy. His vocabulary was too good and we kids didn't have a fighting chance.

My Father wasn't a professionally trained hazzan, but he sang a beautiful Musaf and shared this love with each of his children. We've never been much for leading Shaharis or Kabbalos Shabbos. We sing Musaf, because he sang Musaf. Our niggunim are his niggunim. My Father was a self-taught ba'al koreh and shared this talent with us as well. It took root the best within my oldest brother. My Father also loved to sing zemiros. When I was a little boy, every Shabbos meal was filled with zemiros. For a time he stopped singing on Shabbos when we as teen-agers lost interest. When we returned from college with new tunes and melodies, we were able to get him singing again. He loved learning a new tune, but we loved his niggunim the best. Growing up, I was particularly partial to his tune for Yah Ribbon. When he sang it, it had a wonderful unwritten refrain that included the words, "Tata Zisa Melekh." I always knew that the words were referring to HaShem, but for a little boy who put his Father on a pedestal that was incredibly high, I preferred to think of my Father as the "Tata Zisa," the sweet Father. Years later on the occasion of our Father's 80th birthday, our Mother's 75th birthday, and our parents' 56th wedding anniversary, my brothers and I commissioned a zemer for our parents. On one level, each stanza of the zemer refers to HaShem. On another, more personal level, each stanza referred to a particular Yuntif memory from our parents' home. The zemer was a gift to our parents, but equally so a present to our children to be passed along to their children as a way of remembering and honoring their Bubbie and Zeydie. We sing it every Shabbos and Yuntif. I sang it with my parents during what would turn out to be my Father's last Shabbos. And I attempted unsuccessfully to sing it this past Shabbos as an onein with my children. I couldn't sing through the tears, but my three beautiful daughters sang the zemer in a way that most assuredly elevated my Father's neshamah. My Father lived a full and complete life ... a life of tefillah, Talmud Torah, mitzvos, and hesed. This past August he celebrated his 58th wedding anniversary with my Mother. Although I didn't ask what he gave her as a present, I can guess that it included some form of chocolate, perhaps chocolate covered cherries. They both loved their chocolate covered cherries.

My Father was a devoted and loving Husband and Father. Although he wasn't a person of financial means, we kids never went without. He made sure we each had a Jewish education, but most of what we know came from watching him be the consummate role model. He went to shul, so we went to shul. He loved a good sefer, and we do as well. He had faith in HaShem, so we have faith in HaShem.

In speaking with my brother Danny last night, we both remembered that my Father would frequently say two particular sayings that in many ways summed up his philosophy on life. He would say, "Live and Let Live" and "I don't pasken shailos." When we kids heard him say either of these statements, we always knew what his opinion was on this matter or that. It's just that he wasn't interested in imposing who he was on any of us. He gave us the tools and expected us to make the right decisions.

I have a lifetime of memories to reflect on with my Father, but perhaps my favorite memory was driving with my Father and my brother Danny to a Jewish campground in the country every erev Sukkos at the break of dawn to cut down our own evergreens for skhakh. We'd pile them up in the back seat and trunk of our car and drive them home to our homemade wooden sukkah that my parents would decorate with white sheets and gold foil letters. As I replay the scene in my memory, it wasn't too terribly dissimilar to the description of the Akeidas Yitzhak in the Torah. We got up early in the morning. My Father had his saw in hand. And we drove to a secluded area in the country away from anyone's watchful eyes. Of course, we kids weren't the intended korban, but looking back I can think of so many ways that my parents sacrificed for each of us. To this day when I smell the scent of evergreen, it reminds me of Sukkos in my parents' home.

Pesah was also very memorable in my parents' home. My Father led a great seder that I attempt unsuccessfully to approximate each year. Rather than reflect on a lifetime of Pesah memories, I'll share just one that my Mother mentioned in passing to me the other day. You see, until fairly recently us kids and grandkids would spend the complete Pesah with my parents. When my parents decided that they couldn't host Pesah anymore because it was just too much to do, they decided instead to spend Pesah in various hotel resorts. This past Pesah, my parents decided that it was too much for them to even travel to the hotel. So my Mother, ever the dutiful Eishes Hayil, made Pesah just for the two of them in their own home. According to my Mother, this was the ONLY Pesah they ever spent just as a couple. Even as a young newlywed, my Mother was making Pesah for my Father's elderly parents. Hindsight being what it is, I like to think that this year's Pesah was my Father's intimate gift to my Mother. Time alone. One Pesah just for the two of them. My Father wasn't an effusive man, but his love for my Mother was unquestionable. His love for his children and grandchildren was equally complete. Of course, we spent quite a bit of time talking about my eldest daughter's upcoming Harry Potter themed Bat Mitzvah Party. He was very excited for her and tickled at the idea of the party. Because we knew that he and my Mother wouldn't be able to travel to New York for the Bat Mitzvah, my parents conceded to allowing me to fly to Cincinnati to make a video of them that would be shown at the Bat Mitzvah. Funny man to the end, my Father wrote up a whole speech replete with Harry Potter references. To add to the effect he and my Mother dressed up as wizards for the video. With a twinkle in his eye, you can see in the video how self-satisfied my Father was with his Bat

Mitzvah remarks.

During the last Shabbos my Father and I spent together, his last Shabbos, we spoke about every member of the family. He was extremely proud of each, loved each, and only had good things to say about each. He loved his daughters-in-law and thought of each as his own daughters. He loved each of his grandchildren and was proud to learn of everything each had accomplished and was accomplishing. He loved his sons and spoke warmly of each of us. And he loved my Mother who was his best friend and partner in life these past 58 years.

Personally speaking, I will miss spending time with my Father, calling him on the phone with my latest work accomplishments, or sharing with him the latest news about my wife or daughters, but I must admit to having tremendous comfort in knowing that there weren't any words that were left unsaid between the two of us. He knew how much I loved him and I know how much he loved me.

He will forever be my *"Tata Zisa."*

מְרוֹמְמִי וּמְקַדְּשִׁי הִנְחִילִי שֵׁשֶׁת חַגַּי
אוֹהֲבִי בַּשְּׁבִיעִי הִזְבִּידִי תַּעֲנוּגַי

מוֹצִיאִי קָרָא דְרוֹר עַל קוֹרְאֵי מַעֲמַקִּים
אַמְּצֵנִי עַל כְּנָפָיו נְשָׂאַנִי בַּשְּׁחָקִים
יִשְׁאֲלוּ אַרְבָּעָה מָה הָעֵדָת וְהַחֻקִּים
רַנְּנוּ לַצוּר יִשְׁעֵיכֶם הַחוֹצֵה מֵי אֲפִיקִים

מְרוֹמְמִי וּמְקַדְּשִׁי ...

וְזֹאת הַתּוֹרָה מִמִּדְבָּר מַתָּנָה
גַּבְנֵנִים תְּרַצְדוּן בְּהַנְחִילוֹ אֱמָנָה
וְעָנִינוּ כֻלָּנוּ עֵדוּתוֹ נֶאֱמָנָה
לָקַח טוֹב נָתַן לָנוּ מִשְׁפְּתֵי שׁוֹשַׁנָּה

מְרוֹמְמִי וּמְקַדְּשִׁי ...

דּוֹר וָדוֹר זִכְרוֹ וְאַשְׁרֵי כָּל זוֹכְרָיו
הָמוּ מֵעָיו בְּזָכְרוֹ לְכָתְּנוּ אַחֲרָיו
פְּנֵי מֶלֶךְ לְחַלּוֹת בִּתְקוֹעַ שְׁבָרָיו
רָם יֵשֵׁב בְּכִסְאוֹ בְּפִתְחַ סְפָרָיו

מְרוֹמְמִי וּמְקַדְּשִׁי ...

נֹעַם דְּרָכָיו גֹּדֶל רַחֲמִים
קְרוֹבָה מְחִילָתֵנוּ מְנוֹטֵר כְּרָמִים
לְבֶן בְּגָדִים לְבַקֵּשׁ בַּנְּעִימִים
כְּפוֹר עֲווֹנוֹתֵינוּ מְצוּר עוֹלָמִים

מְרוֹמְמִי וּמְקַדְּשִׁי ...

זִמְרָה וְקוֹל תּוֹדָה בְּאַגּוּד אַרְבָּעָה
בִּזְמַן שִׂמְחָתֵנוּ תִּמְחֶה כָּל דִּמְעָה
אֶדֶר סֻכָּתֵנוּ בְּטֹהַר יְרִיעָה
בְּזָהָב וָכֶסֶף לְקַשְּׁטָהּ כָּל שִׁבְעָה

מְרוֹמְמִי וּמְקַדְּשִׁי ...

תַּמּוּ יְמֵי הֶחָג וְעוֹד יוֹם נֶעֱצָרִים
שְׁלָחָנוּ יַעֲרֹךְ לִשְׁתִילָיו הַיְקָרִים
יַעַן כִּי קָשָׁה פְּרֵדַת טְהוֹרִים
בְּטוֹב דּוֹדָיו יְאָרְחֵם בְּאַהֲבָ דְּבָרִים

מְרוֹמְמִי וּמְקַדְּשִׁי ...

וכתר שם טוב
עולה על גביהן

The crown of
a good name
surpasses
them all.

Pirkei Avos 4:17

He who elevates me and sanctifies me,
bequeathed me my six Festivals.
On the seventh day (Shabbat), He who loves me
gifted me a day of supernal delight.

My Deliverer proclaimed freedom unto those who called out from the depths;
He supported me upon His wings, and carried me aloft unto the skies.
The four [sons] ask, "What are these testimonies and statutes?" [And You reply,]
"Shout out in joyous song to the Rock of your salvation who split the mighty waters!"

He who elevates me and sanctifies me ...

"The Torah He gifted [to us] from amid the barrenness.
The mountains did dance when He bequeathed it as the blueprint [for our lives]."
We answered together, "His Testimony (the Torah) is true!
Goodly teachings were spoken to us from His rose-like lips."

He who elevates me and sanctifies me ...

His impression lasts for all generations, and praiseworthy are those who remember Him.
His feelings are stirred from within as He recalls how we [lovingly] followed after His ways.
The King is beseeched when the shevarim are blown [on the shofar].
He sits enthroned with His books open before Him.

He who elevates me and sanctifies me ...

His ways are of pleasantness, for He is greatly merciful.
Forgiveness is readily granted to us by the Tender of vineyards.
The whitely-garbed one comes to beseech [in Your Sanctuary] with sweetness.
Our misdeeds are pardoned by the Fashioner of the universe.

He who elevates me and sanctifies me ...

Songs of praise and thanksgiving are sung as the four are bound together as one.
This is "The Time of Our Rejoicing" when every last tear is wiped away.
Ensconced is our magnificent sukkah by a curtain of [white] purity;
Adorned with gold and silver for all seven [days].

He who elevates me and sanctifies me ...

The days of the Festive rejoicing conclude, yet we remain [together] another day.
His table He sets for His precious children,
for pained is He by the departure of His pure ones.
He hosts with tender kindnesses and loving words.

He who elevates me and sanctifies me ...

The following letter and peirush (explication) was attached to the *zemer* when it was initially given.

Dear Mom & Dad / Bubbie & Zeydie,

As a measure of our love and admiration, and as a demonstration of our limitless appreciation for everything you have done on our behalf, we pledge to incorporate this *zemer* into our Shabbos and Yom Tov repertoire and pass it down from generation to generation. May you both enjoy the fullness of your years blessed with health, happiness, and *nahas* from your family.

The *piyyut*, מרוממי ומקדשי, was personally commissioned and is being lovingly dedicated to Max and Gloria Frankel by their children and grandchildren on the occasion of their Father's / Zeydie's 80th birthday, their Mother's / Bubbie's 75th birthday, and their Parents' 56th wedding anniversary. On one level, each stanza of the *piyyut* refers to Hashem, as He bestows His people with the joyous Yom Tovim and the beloved gift of Shabbos. This is based on Chapter 23 in *Vayikra* (*Parshas Emor*) wherein the six Yom Tovim (Pesah, Shavuos, Rosh Hashanah, Yom Kippur, Sukkos, and Shemini Atzeres) and Shabbos are described as "*Mikra Kodesh.*" On a deeper and more personal level, the *piyyut* also references various family memories as a way of paying tribute to the Patriarch and Matriarch of the Frankel family. A complete explication follows.

Peirush / Explication

Chorus:

Line 1 refers to the six festivals (ששת חגי) that are explicated across the six stanzas of the *piyyut*. הקב"ה is referred to here as מרוממי ומקדשי, based upon the *nusah* of the festival *kiddush*: ורוממנו מכל לשון וקדשנו במצוותיו.

Line 2 refers to Shabbos. הקב"ה is called אוהבי here ('He who loves me'), recalling the addition of the extra term 'באהבה' in the festival *kiddush* when the festival coincides with a Shabbat. הזבידי means 'he gave to me as a present' (The word זֶבֶד [= gift] appears in Gen. 30:20, and the *paytanim* extended the word with the causative verb תענוגי. (להזביד) recalls the עונג component of Shabbos (cf. Is. 58:13-14: וקראת לשבת ענג '... אז תתענג על ה...').

[Grammatical note: In Biblical Hebrew, the words הנחילי ('he endowed me') and הזבידי ('he gave to me as a gift') would be conjugated with a 'נ' as part of the suffix: הנחילני and הזבידני. However, according to the *paytanic* tradition (represented first and foremost by the *piyyutim* of Elazar b'Rabi Kallir), the 'נ' is an optional component, and may be omitted.]

STANZA 1: PESAH

Line 1 / מוציאי: Hashem, who took us out of Egypt (cf. Ex. 6:7: כי אני ה' אלקיכם המוציא אתכם מתחת סבלות מצרים). granted קרא דרור freedom (the phrase appears in a number of places in *Tanakh*, such as regarding the *Yovel* in Lev. 25:10).

מעמקים קוראי Those who cry out to Hashem from the depths. The phrase is based on Ps. 130:1 (ממעמקים קראתיך ה') and the reference is to *Am Yisrael* crying to Hashem in Egypt (cf. Ex. 2:23: ויזעקו ותעל שועתם אל האלקים מן העבדה).

Line 2 / as a whole refers to Ex. 19:4 (ואשא אתכם על כנפי נשרים.) אמצני: He strengthened me and supported me. נשאני בשחקים: He carried me through the skies. (For the use of the word שחקים as 'skies' see for instance Deut. 33:26).

Line 3 / ארבעה: The four sons, as per the *haggadah*. מה העדת כי ישאלך בנך מחר לאמר מה העדת והחקים. והחקים: as per Deut. 6:20:

Line 4 / רננו לצור ישעיכם: Praise God, your Savior. The phraseology is based on Ps. 95:1: לכו נרננה לה' נריעה לצור ישענו. החוצה מי אפיקים Who divides the mighty waters (the term 'אפיקים' generally refers to lakes and rivers [see for instance Is. 8:7]; however, it can also be used in the sense of 'mighty' and 'strong' [see Job 12:21].)

STANZA 2: SHAVUOT

Line 1 / וזאת התורה: cf. Deut. 4:44: וזאת התורה אשר שם משה לפני בני ישראל. The phrase is from Num. 21:18, which is ממדבר מתנה explained in the Midrash (אותיות דרבי עקיבא, ד"ה דבר אחר סמ"ך) as referring to the giving of the Torah on Sinai: וממדבר מתנה זה מדבר סיני שנתנה להם לוחות במתנה מסיני.

Line 2 / למה תרצדון: cf. Ps. 68:17: למה תרצדון הרים גבננים, which is explained by the Midrash to refer to the clamoring of the mountains who each wished to be the one on which the Torah would be given. See Genesis Rabbah section 100:

למה תרצדון הרים רבים גבנונים... בשעה שבא הקב"ה ליתן תורה בסיני היו ההרים רצים ומדיינים אלו עם אלו, זה אומר עלי התורה ניתנה, וזה אומר עלי תורה ניתנה

בהנחילו אמנה: As Hashem bestowed us with the Torah. אמנה is a term used by the paytanim to refer to the Torah, based upon Prov. 8:30: ואהיה אצלו אמון, and the Midrash in Genesis Rabbah section 1 which interprets that verse as referring to the Torah.

Line 3 / ועננו כולנו: we all answered (at Har Sinai). עדותו נאמנה: The Torah is true (cf. Ps. 19:18: עדות ה' נאמנה ... תורת ה' תמימה).

Line 4 / לקח טוב: cf. Prov. 4:2: כי לקח טוב נתתי לכם תורתי אל תעזבו: Hashem, based on the description of the דוד in משפתי שושנה. Shir Hashirim 5:13: שפתותיו שושנים.

STANZA 3: ROSH HASHANAH

Line 1 / דור ודור זכרו: Hashem (cf. Ex. 3:15: זה זכרי לדר דר). ואשרי כל זוכריו: And fortunate are those who remember You. The idea is based upon the Rosh Hashanah liturgy: אשרי איש שלא ישכחך.

Line 2 / המו מעיו בזכרו לכתנו אחריו: His insides turn as he remembers how we followed Him in the desert. This is based upon two verses from Jeremiah, both included within the זכרונות verses in the liturgy. Jer. 31:19: הבן יקיר לי אפרים ... זכר אזכרנו עוד על כן המו מעי לו; and Jer. 2:2: זכרתי לך חסד נעוריך... לכתך אחרי במדבר.

Line 3 / פני מלך לחלות בתקוע שבריו: Supplicating before the King, as we blow His 'שברים' (that is, as we blow on the shofar as He commanded us).

Line 4 / רם ישב בכסאו: He sits majestically on His chair (cf. Is. 6:1, which his highlighted in the Rosh Hashanah liturgy: יושב על כסא רם בפתח ספריו .(ונשא: as the books of זכרונות are opened before Him.

Stanza 4: Yom Kippur

Line 1 / נעם דרכיו: God's pleasant ways (cf. Prov. 3:17: דרכיה דרכי נעם). גדל רחמים: God's great and bountiful mercy.

Line 2 / קרובה מחילתנו: our forgiveness will soon be granted. מנוטר כרמים: Hashem, whose relationship to Israel is likened to that of a keeper to his vineyard, in the *piyyut* which we sing on Yom Kippur: כי אנו עמך ואתה אלקינו ... אנו כרמיך ואתה נוטרנו.

Line 3 refers to the *Kohen Gadol*, who wears בגדי לבן on Yom Kippur, as he goes into the קדש הקדשים to plead for his nation. (בנעימים) references the היכל and the קדש הקדשים based upon Ps. 27:4: לחזות (בנעם ה' ולבקר בהיכלו).

Line 4 / צור עולמים is Hashem (cf. Is. 26:4: כי ביה ה' צור עולמים).

Stanza 5: Sukkot

Line 1 / זמרה וקול תודה: for the phraseology, cf. Is. 51:3: תודה וקול זמרה. The reference here is to the special joy of Sukkot, about which it is written: ושמחת בחגך (Deut. 16:14).

ארבעה באגוד as we join together the 4 *minim*. The term אגוד references the *halakhah* that the 4 *minim* must be wrapped together (see *Talmud Bavli Sukkah* 11b: לולב צריך אגד)

Line 2 / בזמן שמחתנו: Sukkot, as it is referenced in the liturgy. תִמחה כל דמעה: an expression of eternal Joy based upon Is. 25:8: ומחה ה' אלקים דמעה מעל כל פנים.

Line 3 / אדר סוכתנו בטהר יריעה: The magnificence of our Sukkot, with their clean and beautiful curtains/walls (regarding the importance of beautifying the *sukkah*, see *Talmud Bavli,* Shabbat 133b: התנאה לפניו במצות, עשה לפניו סוכה נאה).

Line 4 refers to the decoration of the *sukkah*.

STANZA 6: SHEMINI ATZERET

Line 1 / וְעוֹד יוֹם נֶעֱצָרִים :תָּמוּ יְמֵי הֶחָג: the days of Sukkot are over. וְעוֹד יוֹם נֶעֱצָרִים yet the people of Israel stay one more day. The term נֶעֱצָרִים is an epithet for those who stay for the עֲצֶרֶת.

Line 2 is based on the description of the essence of Shemini Atzeret as described in *Talmud Bavli Sukkot* 55b, in which this ḥag is likened to a King who sets up a special meal at the end of his celebration just for his loved ones: משל למלך בשר ודם שאמר לעבדיו עשו לי סעודה גדולה, ליום אחרון אמר לאוהבו עשו לי סעודה קטנה כדי שאהנה ממך. The phrase שלחנו יערך recalls Ps. 23:5 (תַּעֲרֹךְ לְפָנַי שֻׁלְחָן), and the word שלחן together with the term שתיליו recalls the image of the children sitting around the father's table, as described in Ps. 128:3: בָּנֶיךָ כִּשְׁתִלֵי זֵיתִים סָבִיב לְשֻׁלְחָנֶךָ.

Line 3 references the language used by Rashi (on Lev. 23:36) to paraphrase the aforementioned *Gemara:* כמלך שזימן את בניו לסעודה לכך וכך ימים, כיון שהגיע זמנן להפטר אמר בני בבקשה מכם עכבו עמי עוד יום אחד, קשה עלי פרידתכם.

Line 4 / בְּטוֹב דּוֹדָיו יְאָרַח: He shall host them with his kind love. בְּאֹהַב דְּבָרִים: with loving words.

THE HIDDEN MEANING OF THE PIYYUT

The first most obvious reference is the acrostic that runs the full-length *piyyut*. The first half of the acrostic presents Max and Gloria Frankel's Hebrew name, Meir v'Golda Frankel (פרנקל וגולדה מאיר). The second half of the acrostic captures the exact date when they sealed their shared destiny on their wedding day, 27 b'Av, 5712 (תשיב באב כז -- corresponding to August 17, 1952). The six stanzas of the *piyyut* present a catalog of spiritual gifts that were bequeathed by Max and Gloria Frankel to their children as well as various scenes drawn from life in the Frankel family.

Stanza 1:

The words מוֹצִיאֵי קְרָא דְרוֹר refers to Max Frankel, who brought forth his children, and who bestowed upon them the gift of freedom. The phrase קוֹרְאֵי מַעֲמַקִּים as the end of line 1 refers to his children sitting at his knees, while line 2 refers to the heights to which he brought them.

Line 3 refers to his four sons, asking questions at his Pesaḥ *seder*, while line 4 is the answer that he provides to them at the *seder* table, as he tells them the story of יציאת מצרים.

Stanza 2:

The first two lines refer to the gift of Torah that Max Frankel bestowed upon his children. Line 1 emphasizes that it is the very same Torah that was given at Sinai that he is passing down to his children, and line 2 refers to his children clamoring to hear his words of Torah. In line 3 the children all respond by saying that his transmission of the Torah is true (עדותו נאמנה). Finally, in line 4, where the Torah is referred to as a לקח טוב, it is worth recalling that in its original context, that phrase refers to the knowledge that a father passes down to his sons (see Prov. 4:1-2: שמעו בנים מוסר אב והקשיבו לדעת בינה: כי לקח טוב נתתי לכם). Additionally, the phrase שפתי שושנה refers according to the *Midrash* to a *Talmid Ḥakham* who recites words of Torah, as per *Midrash Shir Hashirim Rabbah*, section 5: שפתותיו שושנים זה תלמיד חכם הרגיל במשנתו.

Stanza 3:

Line 1 refers to Max Frankel's renown (for his gift of memory). Line 2 references him as a father who lovingly remembers his sons as they follow in his footsteps. Line 3 references his regal countenance as he blows the shofar on Rosh Hashanah. The phrase פני מלך thus no longer serves as the object of the verb לחלות, but rather it is now its subject, and line 3 can therefore be read as follows: פני מלך (that is, Max Frankel standing with his regal countenance), לחלות (as he approaches and pleads), בתקוע שבריו (as he blows out שברים on his *shofar*).

Stanza 4:

Lines 1-2 reference Max Frankel's ways of mercy, and the forgiveness that he dispensed to his children. In line 2, the phrase נוטר כרמים refers to Max Frankel, who tends to his vineyard of children. In line 3, the phrase לבן בגדים references Max Frankel as he wears his white *kittel,* leading services for the *Yamim Noraim,* and requesting forgiveness on behalf of his congregation as described in line 4.

STANZA 5:

In line 1, the phrase אגוד ארבעה refers not only to the gathering together of the four *minim,* but also to Max Frankel as he gathers together his four sons with great joy. In line 3, the phrase טֹהַר יְרִיעָה refers to the white cotton sheets which decorated the inside of the Frankel *sukkah,* and in line 4, the זהב refers to the hand-crafted gold foil letters that adorned the walls with phrases of welcome and blessing.

STANZA 6:

This stanza references the gift of intimacy that Max Frankel shared with each of his children. In this way he is a full embodiment of the משל למלך mentioned in the *Gemara* cited in the commentary above, sharing private time with his children. Also, as noted above, the phraseology in line 2 recalls Ps. 128:3, which portrays sons sitting around a father's table (בניך כשתילי זיתים סביב לשלחניך).

CHORUS:

Finally, the refrain too refers to Max Frankel, who uplifts and blesses his children as he endows them with the legacy of the *ḥagim,* and as he lovingly passes on to them the gift of עונג שבת.